The MILDERS INN of FAIRFIELD, OHIO

The MILDERS INN *of* FAIRFIELD, OHIO

Gangsters, Baseball & Fried Chicken

TERI HORSLEY | Foreword by Tully Milders

Published by American Palate
A Division of The History Press
Charleston, SC
www.historypress.net

Front cover, top left: Greg Lynch/*Journal-News*.

First published 2016

Manufactured in the United States

ISBN 978.1.46711.918.4

Library of Congress Control Number: 2015957668

Notice: The information in this book is true and complete to the best of our knowledge. It is offered without guarantee on the part of the author or The History Press. The author and The History Press disclaim all liability in connection with the use of this book.

This book is dedicated to Tully Milders for sharing his story; to my mother, Margaret Hoel, for her continued encouragement; and to the Lord Jesus Christ, who helped me to find the words whenever life got in the way of the process. I'm grateful to you all.

CONTENTS

Contents

FOREWORD

Growing up, I remember visiting my grandparents on my mother's side in Brookville, Indiana, and I learned from them that my ancestors were farmers, coming here from Germany in the 1820s. Because my mother had many relatives, I learned all about their background. Likewise, on my dad's side, the Milderses were very few. Just my grandparents Ray and Margaret, my aunt and uncle and a couple of great-aunts and uncles were left by the time I arrived. Since I knew so much about my mother's family, I desperately wanted to learn about the Milderses as well. Later, after I started high school, my father suddenly passed away, and it wasn't too many years later that I lost my grandfather Ray, which gave me a deeper desire to research my family tree. I remember before he died, Ray would sing at local restaurants when the family went out to eat, and folks would come up to him and ask about the Milders Inn days. That always made me so proud. Folks would always ask him to sing and share some of the stories about the exciting times at the inn, and I loved hearing about the family history that I knew so little about. I was amazed by the stories about the famous gangsters who visited the inn in the 1930s, and as a baseball fan, it thrilled me when I heard about the many Cincinnati Reds superstars who befriended my grandparents. In fact, two of the Reds players were married at their home. Readers of this book will see that my family's story is a broad one that illustrates much of the American experience as it occurred in the late nineteenth and early twentieth centuries. There truly is something for everyone, as the pages are filled with food, drama, baseball and music.

In addition to connecting me to my own family history, the stories about the Milders Inn also led to my decision to follow in my family's footsteps as a restaurateur. Having been in the industry for over thirty years, it is with utmost personal pride that I strive today to serve my diners with the same quality, value, great service and pleasant environment that made the Milders Inn famous. It is also with true passion that I continue to fry my great-grandmother Mom Milders's chicken each Monday night at Hamilton's Ryan's Tavern, a restaurant that in many ways is similar to the Milders Inn. I still use Mom's original iron skillets, and I still share the many stories handed down to me from my aunt Petie, who worked hard to keep the memories of our family alive. Today, even my mother, Marlene Milders Sloneker, assists me each week in the preparation of Mom's fried chicken, and we love to reminisce about many of the stories from our past. Now that my own son has followed in my footsteps by embarking on a restaurant career of his own, it is my hope that he will carry on the tradition and share the Milders Inn stories with future generations of our family. It is also my hope that in addition to exploring my family's story, this book will inspire readers to spend some time delving into their own family histories so that, like me, they can learn about their own present circumstances as they are defined by their past.

TULLY MILDERS

ACKNOWLEDGEMENTS

Thanks to the following:
Tully Milders.
Marlene Milders Sloneker.
Don and Vickie Ryan and the staff of Ryan's Tavern.
The extended Milders family.
Alisha Lilley, the owner of Captured Beauty Photography, for her excellent eye and beautiful photos.
Journal News photographer Greg Lynch for always being a true professional.
And a special thanks to Margaret Hoel for her support throughout the entire creative process.

PROLOGUE

On May 27, 1929, at approximately 6:15 p.m., noted Hamilton gangster Joseph "Turkey Joe" Jacobs was having dinner at the Milders Inn along with gang leader and alleged murderer Bob Zwick. It's believed the two were enjoying Mom Milders's famous fried chicken, as they so often did when dining at the restaurant. Suddenly, in the middle of their meal, they saw a suspicious brown sedan drive past heading west on what is now Fairfield's Nilles Road. Leaving their chicken on their plates, the two gangsters ran from the inn and jumped into a green Nash that was parked outside. They took off after the mysterious car. Though no one ever knew why they were determined to catch up with the sedan, it was suspected that they wanted to end a long-running gang war by setting up a joint bootleg liquor deal.

With Zwick behind the wheel and Jacobs in the passenger seat, the two lost sight of the sedan and eventually gave up their chase. Zwick then pulled into an abandoned field behind the Symmes Corner School so they could plan their next move. At around 7:00 p.m., as the two sat between the wheat and high corn, shots suddenly rang out and a deadly ambush was underway. Zwick and Turkey Joe hadn't noticed that the infamous brown sedan had crept up behind them, blocking their exit from the field. As the ensuing machine gun fire ripped through the night, Turkey Joe Jacobs took the brunt of the attack and was shot sixteen times, with eleven bullets hitting him in the head. He died instantly. Bob Zwick, meanwhile, managed to get out of the car and crawl into a ditch, where he hid out and assessed his own injuries. With bullet wounds in his skull and hips and two of his fingers now gone, Zwick decided to make his way back to the Milders Inn, where his girlfriend, Dago Rose Meyer, worked as a waitress.

After staggering out of the field to the road, Zwick hijacked a car by jumping onto its running board and pulled a gun on the female driver. According to the Milders family, it was at this point that the terrified woman gave in to his demands and took him back to the restaurant, where he staggered inside and where Mom's fried chicken was still on his plate. With the police and killers now hot on Zwick's tail, his girlfriend helped him into the kitchen so they could begin planning his escape. As they arrived in the back, legend has it that Mom Milders was still frying chicken for the remaining crowd in the dining room. Weighing over three hundred pounds, Mom sat on a stool while she cooked, her large skirt covering the floor around her. As Bob Zwick approached, she remained seated, and without saying a word, she lifted up her skirt and Zwick crawled underneath. Mom reportedly let the gangster remain there until the police left and he was able to make his escape.

The next day, it was business as usual as there were customers to serve and chickens to fry. The events of the previous night were forgotten, and though there are several different versions of the story, eyewitnesses at the inn confirmed that Turkey Joe Jacobs and Bob Zwick were dining together there shortly before the shootings occurred. But with Jacobs now dead and Zwick long gone, it was time for the Milderses and their employees to get back to work. Though it may seem strange that the drama wasn't devastating for all those involved, the reality is that it wasn't. In fact, for the staff at the Milders Inn, drama and celebrity amidst the backdrop of great food was just another example of a typical day in their lives.

Part I
The Early Years

Chapter 1

JAKE

1850–1869

In the mid-nineteenth century, over one and a half million immigrants arrived in America, with most coming from Germany, England, Ireland and Holland. For the Dutch, the 1840s were known as the "Great Migration," as thousands fled their homeland due to religious tension brought about by a government-backed movement away from Calvinism. This perceived attack on their freedom of worship, combined with the economic hardship brought about by the failure of the rye and potato crops, saw many Dutch citizens looking to the United States as the land of religious freedom and prosperity. As a result, one of the largest immigration movements in American history began, and upon arrival here, most of the Dutch settled in small coastal towns in the East or in the Midwest, where a new sense of community and family flourished. Meanwhile, from the American perspective, President Zachary Taylor strongly supported immigration, particularly by those with German and Dutch heritage. Upon taking over his office, Taylor believed that German and Dutch intellectuals and liberal reformers would benefit his presidency through their commitment to freedom of worship, and this was a commitment that meshed well with American values at the time. Likewise, with a military background and no previous political experience, Taylor proved to be ill prepared for the rising tensions brought about by the slavery issue that ultimately led to the Civil War, and he thought the convictions of the immigrants would help him make political points here in America.

Though his assumptions were incorrect, Taylor's acceptance of immigration allowed for the growth of many of America's early Dutch communities that remain today, including several that remain in and around Hamilton, Ohio.

One of those disenchanted immigrants who arrived in America in search of a better life was Peter Milders, a stocky man who came to Hamilton from Holland in 1850, the same year that President Taylor died. Hamilton, founded in 1791 by European Americans with backgrounds that were similar to Milders's, first served as a supply station for the troops of General Arthur Sinclair and General Anthony Wayne. Named after U.S. founding father Alexander Hamilton, what was first known as Fort Hamilton was abandoned by 1800, and the city was then platted and a local government seated by 1803. By 1810, Hamilton had been incorporated by the Ohio General Assembly but lost its status in 1815 when the city refused to hold elections. The city reincorporated in 1827 but this time included Rossville, which was located across the Great Miami River that bordered the city. It was the inclusion of Rossville that would later prove profitable for the members of Peter Milders's family.

Though not much is known about Milders's life before he arrived here, we do know that after being educated in his homeland, he grew into a hardworking businessman with high intelligence and great talent, making him just the type of person the president, and Hamilton's citizenry, welcomed. Peter's first business venture was the purchase of a bakery that he operated on Third near Canal Street, and because of his giftedness, it quickly became profitable. By the early 1860s, Milders's success was comparable to that of many Hamilton businessmen, as the city was nationally known by this point as a major manufacturing entity. In fact, Hamilton held such a prominent place in the national arena that on September 17, 1859, future president Abraham Lincoln visited the city to support fellow Republican and Ohio gubernatorial candidate William Dennison. Lincoln's appreciation for Hamilton as it tied to the concept of "popular sovereignty" (a state where a government is created and supported by its people) was noted in the very first line of his speech, and it typified the belief system of Peter Milders and other Hamiltonians with similar values. "This beautiful and far-famed Miami Valley is the garden spot of the world," Lincoln said shortly after arriving at the train station, a spot that remains on Hamilton's preservation list today.

While Lincoln did not spend much time in Hamilton, it was during his visit that he was first mentioned as a possible candidate for president, creating more political power for those local candidates who showed their support. While it's not known if Peter Milders attended Lincoln's speech, this change in direction for the future president came at the same time that a change was brewing for Milders. Having proven his success as a baker, Milders became restless and was ready to reinvent himself. As a result, he decided to pursue other opportunities, and when another local Dutch immigrant approached him asking for a job, Milders saw his way out of the kitchen. After meeting Valentine Ruhl, Milders, instead of hiring him, talked Ruhl into buying the bakery for $300. As a result of the sale, Milders's commercial baking days were over, and his exit from the bakery left time for personal exploration. His deep concern about the local need for news from the Civil War prompted him to fill that need, and he started the *Hamilton Daily Democrat*, a newspaper that eventually became the *Journal News* of today. As publisher of the newspaper, Milders spent his days reporting the news about local soldiers who were fighting on the front lines. With a deep desire for serving the community he now loved, Peter Milders also became Hamilton's postmaster sometime toward the end of the century.

Though successful in all these endeavors, it was family that mattered most to Milders, the result of his having married Hamilton native Margaret Rupp after a serious courtship during his bakery days. It was during the early years of the marriage that Margaret Rupp Milders gave birth to seven children, including their son Jacob, born on March 25, 1869. It's at this point, with the birth of Jacob Milders, that the long and winding road to the Milders Inn begins.

1869–1906

As a boy, Jacob Milders had no plans to own a restaurant. However, with his father's success and love of community, Jacob, known to his family as Jake, was destined to be a man of the same immense talent and versatility enjoyed by Peter. When Jake was a boy, the Milders family typified the nineteenth-century midwestern home. Both parents were married and living under the same roof; the children were loved and not considered property, as was the case for many Americans in the early 1800s; and Jake Milders was expected to work around the house when he wasn't attending class at the Hamilton City Schools. By the time Jake reached adulthood, the city of Hamilton had become a beacon of prosperity, growing into an even larger manufacturing center than it was when his father, Peter, was young. As Milders began to make a name for himself in the local business community, Hamilton was recognized for the production of farm equipment like reapers, hay cutters, threshers and steam engines, as well as machine tools, house hardware, saws for mills, paper, papermaking machinery, carriages, guns and woolen goods. This industrial success for the city set the stage for local businessmen like Jake Milders to open small retail shops. Ultimately, community prosperity meant personal prosperity, and as such, money was readily available for the buying and selling of goods and services. As a result, Jake Milders was in the perfect position by the time he reached early adulthood to become a major local success, as he inherited his father's quick mind, strong work ethic and stocky physique, making him quite capable of doing his part to serve the city as well.

First, Jake worked in the mail business and then at the local newspaper, where he spent seventeen years as the circulation manager. While working at the paper, he also began to cultivate his love of baseball, which made sense considering his strong business acumen and commitment to reporting the news of the day. Baseball and Jake Milders basically grew up together, with the sport seeing a huge rise in popularity during this time after the Civil War. With the establishment of both the National and American Leagues by the turn of the century, and the subsequent establishment of the World Series in 1903, the economic benefit of baseball was attractive to a businessman like Jake Milders, so he worked hard to promote Hamilton's local baseball park, which he eventually bought. Likewise, his interest in developing baseball in Hamilton came about as a result of the success of the Cincinnati Red Stockings (later becoming the Cincinnati Reds), located just twenty-eight miles south of town. The Red Stockings had the historical distinction of becoming America's first official all-professional team in 1869, having been organized in 1866. With the Red Stockings making a twenty-one-game, undefeated eastern sweep in their first professional year, folks across the entire region developed a passion for the game, so it was no coincidence that a smart businessman like Jake Milders decided to capitalize on baseball fever. As he worked to develop the sport in Hamilton, Jake's love of the game continued to grow, and it was baseball that would ultimately change his life, as he created a connection to the sport and the Reds for future generations of his family.

Over the next twenty-five years, Jake built a total of four baseball parks in Hamilton, including Krebs Park on High Street and a park in Lindenwald where the Hamilton Browns played and that later became Benninghoffen Park. Both teams were semi-professional, although several major leaguers got their start on their rosters. Krebs Park was Jake's biggest baseball success story, being noted as one of the first ballparks in the region to have night games, although the accomplishment wasn't without a few problems. Reportedly, the first time Milders turned on the lights at Krebs Park, half of Hamilton was blacked out from the power surge. But Milders eventually got the lighting problem fixed, and with his successful baseball parks up and running, Jake, like his father, Peter, continued to expand his business interests. He next bought the Wedge postcard shop on Third Street. His love of baseball once again dominated his business life, and in addition to running the postcard shop, he also organized and served as the manager of its baseball team, which became part of Hamilton's Industrial League. With a need for variety and an innate knowledge of how to achieve success, Jake also bought a second postcard and novelty shop and, along with his growing business career, expanded into community service and tourism. He served five years on the Hamilton School Board and developed the Hamilton Bathing Beach, a popular resort along the Great Miami River, north of town.

One of the keys to Jake Milders's success was his kind personality and delightful sense of humor, qualities that would serve him well in later years at the Milders Inn. In fact, Jake was one of the first Hamilton businessmen who willingly poked fun at himself when, in 1911, he allowed the authors of a locally published caricature book to include him in their roast. Politically, Jake Milders was a staunch Democrat and very active in the local party. In addition, his commitment to public service led him to join several fraternal organizations, including Esther Court No. 4, the Tribe of Ben-Hur. Though now extinct, the Tribe of Ben-Hur was an early twentieth-century organization based on the novel *Ben-Hur* whose members were chosen based on their strict moral, religious and patriotic beliefs, characteristics that clearly defined Jake Milders. During the peak of his career, Jake also joined Butler Aerie No. 407 of the Fraternal Order of Eagles and the Hamilton Elks, two organizations that are still active in Hamilton today.

Like his father, Jake Milders was a devoted family man, having married Mary A. Doellman in 1891. Though the backgrounds of homemakers were not as important to nineteenth-century historians, we do know that Mary Doellman was the daughter of a prominent Hamilton couple, Frank and Anna (Heet) Doellman, and she was the eldest of eleven children, born on June 9, 1872. Her father, Frank, born just twenty-one years before his daughter, was a German immigrant, and upon arriving here with his wife, Anna, a homemaker, he worked as a boilermaker according to both the 1880 census

Hamilton's Krebs baseball team, circa 1908. A young Ray Milders is serving as the team batboy. *Tully Milders family photo.*

Jake Milders's Hamilton Wedge baseball team. *Tully Milders family photo.*

A caricature of Jake Milders in a 1911 Hamilton Chamber of Commerce publication about prominent local businessmen. *Tully Milders family photo.*

Jake Milders's Elks Lodge induction photo. *Tully Milders family photo.*

and the 1900 census. Frank Doellman's was a dangerous job that was in demand, thanks to Hamilton's emergence as a large industrial center and the specialization required to perform a boilermaker's duties. Doellman spent his days filling large metal containers with toxic liquids and waste, and because of the danger, he earned approximately $1,979.60 a year, which is comparable to $56,560 today. In comparison, the average American worker in 1900 earned $438 per year, so life at the Doellmans' Hamilton Fifth Ward home was more privileged than most. As a result, Frank and Anna Doellman raised their children in a style that would eventually be reflected in the interior of the Milders Inn, and they worked especially hard to teach their daughter Mary to appreciate the finer things of life. After spending the remaining years of their lives committed to hard work, faith and family, Frank Doellman died on August 16, 1916, and Anna followed many years later, on March 7, 1938. Both are buried in Hamilton's St. Stephens Cemetery.

Meanwhile, as the Doellmans' daughter Mary (who later became known as "Mom") grew into adulthood and married Jake Milders, she eventually gave birth to two children: Helen in 1892 and Ray in 1901. Jake, in his devotion to Mary and his kids, included them in most of his business and sports ventures, even allowing his small son Ray to serve as batboy on his various baseball teams. Continuing the family tradition of business success and community service, Jake and Mom's daughter, Helen, after reaching adulthood, served as the assistant secretary of the Hamilton Chamber of Commerce, as an influential member of the Hamilton Food Conservation Movement and as a participant in many local Red Cross drives. Sadly, Helen Milders died at the young age of thirty-nine, seven years before her father, Jake. Meanwhile, Ray Milders, after reaching adulthood, also became an important figure in Hamilton during the first half of the twentieth century, growing into a gifted athlete, musician and successful businessman at the future Milders Inn.

1906–1913

With successful baseball parks, booming small businesses and satisfying political and community service involvement, one might think that Jake Milders had time to relax while enjoying his success. By this time, Hamilton's industrial image had skyrocketed, and the city was now internationally known as a heavy manufacturing center, specializing in the production of vaults, safes, machine tools, cans for vegetables, paper, papermaking machinery, locomotives, frogs and switches for railroads, steam engines, diesel engines, printing presses and automobile parts. In fact, Hamilton's Mosler Safe Company, founded in 1867, built the vault that originally housed the Declaration of Independence and the United States Constitution, so Jake Milders's rise to success came at the same time that Hamilton's success was making headlines around the world.

With the huge opportunity for business advancement in the booming city, Jake Milders did not stop to relax on the heels of his previous success; instead, he recognized that hardworking Hamiltonians needed an entertainment and sports venue where they could relax after a long day on the job. As a result, one of Jake's most significant accomplishments came in 1906, when he became the primary force behind the promotion and construction of a large arena that sat on B Street between Park and Wayne Avenues. The building, known as the Coliseum, seated 1,800 and measured 115 feet by 85 feet, bigger than anything else in the region. It was designed by noted Hamilton contractor J. Conrad Rigler. Milders co-owned the Coliseum with local businessmen F.M. Heck, Ray Wortendike, Mike Kane and C.E. Heiser. The Coliseum was the only place in town where roller polo (now known as rink hockey) was played, and the Hamilton team eventually became part of the National Roller Polo League, founded in Dayton, Ohio, in 1882. The sport was known by this name because the skaters simulated polo in their matches but used wooden floors and manpower instead of horses and ice. The Coliseum's playing floor further demonstrated the building's massive size, as it was 50 by 100 feet, with seats built from floor to roof in an amphitheater style. The east end of the great hall had a balcony where bands played, and the polo teams' dressing rooms were beneath, adding a sense of style and functionality. The main part of the arena had numerous windows so the outside light could shine through, as well as ten large incandescent arc lights and five hundred small lights so games could be played at night. Nothing like the Coliseum had ever been built in Hamilton, and according to historian Jim Blount, nothing like roller polo had ever been played:

> *A crowd of 2000 (over capacity) was on hand that first night, (January 23, 1906), and before the polo match, a basketball game was played pitting the Coliseum team against the Cincinnati, Hamilton and Dayton Railroad team from Cincinnati. Hamilton won 39–6. The emcee was Miller Huggins, the second baseman for the Reds, who was later inducted into the Reds Hall of Fame.*

Blount, in his 1991 article for the *Hamilton Journal News*, added that a night at the Coliseum was one of prestige and excitement for all, and with guests like Miller Huggins, the Milderses' later connection to the Cincinnati Reds continued to develop. One never knew who they would see at the Coliseum, and that, combined with the popularity of roller polo, often made it impossible for Jake Milders and his staff to accommodate everyone who wanted a ticket. Because of his success, Jake's entrepreneurial spirit and the love of his many hobbies took over, and he decided to host other popular events at the Coliseum, including regular basketball games, dog and poultry shows for families, dances and political speeches. One of the most significant political events in Hamilton history actually occurred at the Coliseum in 1912, when William Jennings Bryan—on behalf of then presidential candidate Woodrow Wilson—outlined the future president's platform before a packed house.

THE 1913 FLOOD

By the dawn of 1913, life couldn't have been better for Hamilton and for Jake Milders and his family. People came from across the region to enjoy the many events at the Coliseum, his baseball parks continued to attract area fans and his family life was on track, with his wife and two children keeping him happy at home. However, as is often the case, life changed dramatically for both the city and Jake Milders in the spring of 1913, when the worst weather disaster in Hamilton's history leveled the city and much of Jake's life. It was March 21 of that year—coincidentally, Good Friday—a day that started out ideally across Hamilton and the entire state of Ohio. Temperatures were a balmy seventy degrees, a welcome relief after a winter of heavy rain that left severely saturated ground. Suddenly, an Arctic cold front approached the state, and temperatures dropped fifty degrees in six hours, with ninety-mile-an-hour winds reported in Toledo alone. For four days, rain battered Ohio, with most areas reporting at least eight inches of water on severely flooded streets.

Between March 21 and 24, the weather wasn't horrible in Hamilton, but by March 25, the storm had hit with a vengeance, and life for those who survived would never be the same. Within twenty-four hours, all four of Hamilton's bridges—Black Street, High/Main Street, Columbia and the Railroad Bridge—washed away as floodwaters rose, literally splitting the town in two. Three hundred buildings were destroyed in one day, and two thousand others had to be razed because of the damage. Over two hundred Hamiltonians lost their lives in the destruction, either through drowning, through suicide from the overwhelming loss that permeated the region or through diseases that came during the aftermath of the devastation. Water in downtown Hamilton rose to eight feet in places and up to eighteen feet from Fifth Street to what is now the South Hamilton Crossing on State Route 127. The water's rise was so fast that people were forced to run to their attics for safety, and then as the water continued to climb, they were forced to break through their roofs to escape. In addition to the dead, over one thousand horses drowned, as well as other livestock and pets, and raw sewage tainted the rising waters, making it impossible to drink. Nearly one-third of the population—close to ten thousand people—was left homeless. Jim Blount, in his book *Butler County's Greatest Weather Disaster—March 1913*, wrote: "For many survivors of the 1913 flood, the emotional scars remained for a lifetime. Terrifying flood memories caused people to turn their backs on [memories that occurred before] the flood."

As bewildered Hamiltonians tried to pick up the remnants of their shattered lives, one of those forced to change the entire course of his life was a devastated Jake Milders. As the high floodwaters ripped through Hamilton's streets, the Coliseum floated off its foundation, dumping the remains of the building into the Great Miami River. The city's most popular entertainment venue was torn to shreds as it floated downstream and crashed into one of the covered bridges that fell. But the devastation for

Jake Milders didn't stop with this one loss. Krebs field was now gone, and Jake's two downtown novelty stores were destroyed in the flood, leaving him emotionally distraught and financially ruined within the span of twenty-four hours. Years later, in a 1978 letter to Fairfield historian Esther Benzing, it was clear that the memory of the 1913 flood still haunted Milders's son, Ray, who was near the end of his own life by that point, yet he still carried the emotional scars that he received as a twelve-year-old boy: "My parents were wiped out [financially] overnight. After the flood, [Hamilton mayor] John Holzberger came to my dad and asked him to buy a small café [the Village Café and Summer Garden] in Fairfield Township. [Still in a state of shock,] my dad said, 'With what?'"

Ray Milders said Mayor Holzberger took his dad to the Hamilton Citizen Bank not long after the flood wiped him out, and because of Jake's solid reputation in the community, the bank president loaned him the money to start over. With that, Jake Milders was forced to put his personal pain behind him, and he was successful in doing what so many flood survivors were not. He dug deep and pulled himself up for the sake of his family. By so doing, he chose success over failure, laying the groundwork for the next phase of his life and the birth of the Milders Inn.

Chapter 2

A NEW DIRECTION

In 1914, just one year after the Hamilton, Ohio area was devastated by the great flood, another devastation of sorts occurred at the Village Café and Summer Garden, in the nearby suburb of Fairfield Township. The township, one of thirteen in Butler County and one of the first five in the area, lies in the county's south-central section, about three miles south of Hamilton. Fairfield Township was erected by the Court of Quarter Sessions on May 10, 1803, around the same time that Hamilton became a city. The Village Café and Summer Garden was located in the Symmes Corner neighborhood of the township, at what is now the corner of Pleasant Avenue and Nilles Road. The intersection today is part of the city of Fairfield. Before the flood, H.J. Meyers owned and had early success at the café, but he was looking to sell it by 1914, as it was run-down and had a horrible reputation because of the thugs who had started hanging out there. On the plus side, with the restaurant's location at Symmes Corner, it was near the trolley line that ran between Cincinnati to the south and Dayton to the north. The Cincinnati and Dayton Line, as it was known, was built around 1900 and provided fast passenger and freight service, with a stop outside the restaurant's front door. Having a local stop on a trolley line meant folks with money had access to local businesses and restaurants when they needed to eat, so the trolley contributed greatly to the growth of what is now Fairfield, as well as to downtown Hamilton and ultimately to the Village Café and soon-to-be Milders Inn. Likewise, a second trolley, the Mill Creek Valley Line, provided two-hour service from Hamilton to Cincinnati, with fares costing

The exterior of the Milders Inn with the enclosed garden visible on side of the building and the trolley tracks out front. *Tully Milders family photo.*

only a nickel for adults and three cents for children. The Mill Creek Line also proved beneficial for the restaurant, as it stopped on what is now State Route 4, only a mile away.

Though unincorporated, Symmes Corner was also a well-known settlement, having been heavily developed by the early twentieth century. Landowners began arriving as early as 1836, forty-one years after Celadon Symmes was given his choice of one square mile of ground owned by his uncle, Judge John Cleves Symmes. Celadon was given the ground because he was a devoted overseer of his uncle's farm on North Bend Road in Cincinnati, and he wanted to develop an area in the untapped resources to the north. In 1795, Symmes chose the area bounded by what is now Symmes Road to the north, Pleasant Avenue to the west, Nilles Road to the south and Dixie Highway to the east. At the time, the ground was valued at $800. The construction of churches marked the first stage of development at Symmes Corner sometime around 1837, and homes, stores and restaurants started appearing in the 1840s. Though the exact construction date of the Village

A drawing of the Milders Inn, circa 1970, by Tully Milders. *Captured Beauty Photography.*

Café and Summer Garden is not known, it's believed it was built during this period of expansion.

Meanwhile, after receiving the bank loan from Hamilton's Citizen Bank, Jake Milders arrived at Symmes Corner and, per the request of Hamilton's mayor, bought the Village Café and Summer Garden. Prior to his arrival in Fairfield Township, Jake, Mary and their two children lived their entire lives in Hamilton because of his business connections to the city. When he purchased the restaurant, Jake moved his family to an apartment upstairs, and his first order of business was to rename the restaurant the Milders Inn. Many years later, Milders's son, Ray, who eventually took over ownership of the inn, told Esther Benzing that buying the Village Café was a major endeavor for his parents:

> *Their first project was to get rid of the undesirables and start building a better clientele. After months of hard work, they were really attracting the finest people in the area and from as far away as Dayton, Richmond, Indianapolis and Middletown. They enjoyed a fine business until* [a slowdown during] *the 1930 Depression. For the record, Prohibition set in in 1919 and carried through until 1935. Afterward, we had another complete remodeling, and from then on business was* [once again] *great.*

Milders remarked that while the inn wasn't, in his opinion, "the prettiest place in the world," he felt his parents made it into a top-notch restaurant with the "finest food and the finest clientele to be had anywhere." Likewise, in October 1981, *Fairfield Sun* writer Mable Kohler Holbrock corroborated Ray's story when she reported the reason behind Jake Milders's decision to completely overhaul the restaurant right from the start: "The second night two men got into a rough fight. Jake decided at that point that he didn't want to run that kind of business and he decided to cater to what he called a better class of people. He charged higher prices [immediately] to attract a more elite clientele."

THE DÉCOR

Though Jake's son, Ray, didn't consider the Milders Inn to be the prettiest place around, after his father remodeled, his mother's sophisticated upbringing took over, and she took great care to adorn it with the finest of amenities. All tables in the revamped dining room were inlaid with mother of pearl and covered with white linen tablecloths, and the napkins were cloth instead of paper, no doubt a result of Mom and her Doellman family influence. In 1981, Esther Benzing remembered that in addition to her enjoyment of the tasteful décor, a trip to the Milders Inn meant great service for the customer: "It was nice to be greeted at the door every time you went there to eat. The hospitality shown to the Milderses' patrons was second to none."

With the décor in place, the Milderses began to hire staff, ending up with seven female German cooks and numerous waitresses. Since Mom Milders was German and immigration played such an important role in the development of the surrounding region, including the settlement of the nearby German neighborhood of Lindenwald, it made sense that the Milderses looked first to their neighbors to fill open positions on their staff. Though the nineteenth century saw many Germans facing severe discrimination in Greater Cincinnati and Hamilton as the natives felt they were responsible for taking their jobs, the Milderses' own heritage led them to share their success with the descendants of their homelands. However, though they were kind to their help, the Milderses expected their staff to work hard, as was evident when Esther Benzing interviewed one of the granddaughters of employee Ola Ludwig Baker. She said that her grandmother regularly stood for hours ironing the dining room tablecloths,

Inside the dining area of the Milders Inn. *Tully Milders family photo.*

as Mom Milders demanded that they make a perfect presentation for her dinner guests.

As an aside, though it is unlikely that Mom Milders tried to make any kind of feminist statement as she took over her role at the Milders Inn, her duties as kitchen manager, head chef and decorator came at a unique time for women in America. World War I broke out in 1914, the same year that the Milders Inn opened. Suddenly, women across the country were forced to leave their roles as homemakers, filling jobs vacated by men who were headed into battle. Mom Milders had a similar fate, too, as she was forced into working outside the home so that her family could recover from the 1913 flood. Though Mom's role could be viewed as more traditionally female than some, it came at a time when women began serving in many nontraditional capacities, including as factory workers, doctors, lawyers and bankers. As such, Mom Milders played a pivotal role in the local women's rights movement, as she hired homemakers who needed jobs, making life at the Milders Inn a microcosm of what was happening around the globe.

Jake Milders standing in front of the Milders Inn on the trolley tracks. *Tully Milders family photo.*

With the inside of the inn established and the staff in place, the Milderses next began work on a special area outside known as the garden. Located on the south side of the property, the garden was a fenced-in patio for those who wanted to eat outdoors. There was a huge tree in the center of the patio that was left in place to keep customers cool in the summer, and several pedestal fans adorned the area, constantly pumping in fresh air. In the fall, a large canvas was stretched around the garden's fence to keep out the cold. The patio accommodated up to 150 people and was often used for wedding receptions and other community events. "People loved this area of the inn, for in those days there was no air conditioning, and it was such a refreshing place to dine," Ray Milders later said.

Likewise, a sign on the front of the building near the garden read: "THE BEST IN THE MIDDLE WEST," serving as a testament to the delightful outdoor seating area, as well as to the food and service offered inside.

The Food

Though it was the décor that impressed people when they first arrived at the Milders Inn, it was the quality of the food that kept them coming back. While Mom Milders was particular when it came to the layout of the restaurant, she could be considered obsessive when it came to food preparation, earning her the reputation of being both a great and demanding cook. Food temperature, cuts of meat and freshness were of utmost importance to Mom, and she wouldn't compromise when it came to these aspects of her cooking. Fortunately for the Milderses' patrons, Mom's high standards were responsible for the inn's most popular dishes, which included fried chicken, chicken sandwiches, ham, roast beef and Mom's locally famous chicken potpie. Likewise, hamburgers were never served, as Mom considered them too common for the clientele she wanted to attract. Though the years between 1914 and 1920 were the same in which hamburgers actually gained their popularity in America, they appealed to the working poor, and that was a group that likely could not have afforded the cost of dining at the Milders Inn. As for the aforementioned food temperature, Mom again wouldn't compromise, and everything was served directly from the oven, meaning that traditional family-style vegetables like mashed potatoes were made in very small quantities so they would always be fresh. All pies that were served for dessert were baked daily, and everything that came out of the inn's kitchen had to be "hot," not "warm," meaning some diners had to wait up to three hours for their meals to be served: "People didn't mind waiting [to be served], for they loved those chicken dinners," Ray Milders later said.

Mom's great-grandson Tully Milders, who still serves her fried chicken today at Hamilton's Ryan's Tavern, said he prepares it in advance because his clientele is not willing to wait for more than a few minutes, let alone for three hours, for their food. Though Tully wouldn't give away the names of the spices that he uses in the family chicken recipe, he said that the secret to its delicious taste is connected to the cast-iron skillets and the temperature of the lard that Mom Milders fried it in:

> *One of the most important things I learned about Mom Milders's fried chicken was how to prepare the lard. To get the proper taste, you need to first heat it so that it is half melted, or half liquid and half solid. This is the point at which you begin to fry the chicken, and if the lard melts beyond this before you drop in the meat, the chicken won't taste right. In addition, Mom had eight iron skillets full of chicken frying at the same time, which*

Mom Milders's fried chicken and home-grown side dishes, an example of the original plating at the Milders Inn in 1914. This dish was being served at Ryan's Tavern on Milders Inn night in 2015. *Captured Beauty Photography.*

Mom Milders's original cast-iron skillets awaiting her chicken. *Captured Beauty Photography.*

Above: Mom Milders's original cast-iron skillets, 1914. *Captured Beauty Photography.*

Right: Mom Milders's original kitchen scale, 1914. *Captured Beauty Photography.*

made it easier for her to serve many people at once. I still use those skillets and Mom's original food scale to weigh the meat when I fry her chicken for my customers today.

In addition to their being willing to wait for three hours to enjoy the quality of the food served at the Milders Inn, patrons of the restaurant were often traveling to Cincinnati or Dayton as a result of the trolley that stopped outside. Since this was the typical mode of travel in America in the late '10s and early 1920s, folks had more time to kill as they waited for the next trolley to pick them up, and as such, they took longer to dine than people do today. With that being the case, it made sense that the Milders's customers were willing to wait a long while for their food. Likewise, fast food as we know it didn't become popular for another thirty years, until the 1950s, and since quality mattered when it came to fine dining, waiting for the food to be prepared to perfection was just part of the overall experience at the Milders Inn. In addition, most of the customers who lived nearby were immigrants, and they had an appreciation for fried chicken and home-grown vegetables because that was the comfort food they grew up with. As a result, it was appropriate for the Milderses to serve their favorite foods, no matter how long it took to prepare them. Though it's not known exactly where the Milders Inn fried chicken recipe came from, Jake and Mom's own Dutch and German family background likely played at least a small part in the creation of their most popular dish and accompanying vegetables, since, like their neighbors, they, too, grew up enjoying the comfort food that was defined by these dishes. In addition, because of their European background, cooking was a family affair for the Milderses, and though Mom was ahead of her time as the head chef, her husband, Jake, also pitched in when it came to training the staff: "It was Dad who taught the girls to fry the chicken, and the girls under Mom's direction canned over two thousand cans of corn each summer, which was served all winter. The inn also had homemade noodles that the staff made with the chicken broth," said Ray Milders in a 1978 interview in the *Fairfield Sun.*

Mom Milders relied on the process of canning for more than just corn each summer, as in her mind, an elite clientele meant that vegetables must be fresh all year. The canning of the produce became a massive project for Mom and her employees, as they also prepared thirty-five thousand homemade pickles and many gallons of catsup, homemade relishes, preserves and tomato juice. The Milderses hired fifteen additional women just for the canning project, and Ray Milders told the *Fairfield Sun* that customers came from over one hundred miles away just to enjoy the inn's delicious produce: "They had a customer in Indianapolis who came all that distance just to enjoy that delicious corn, though Mom would never serve yellow corn because, in her opinion, yellow corn was 'horse corn.'"

The complete chicken dinners cost $1.00, which is approximately $11.48 today. The dinner included half of a three-pound bird, mashed potatoes and gravy, the fresh vegetables that were grown on the Milderses' property (a large field behind the inn), a choice of slaw or salad, fresh fruit cocktail, hot biscuits with butter (again, her high standards figured in as Mom Milders refused to serve margarine because she also considered it to be too common) and fresh pie or cake for dessert. One of the German cooks who worked in the kitchen had a special flair for making biscuits and pies, so that was the extent of her work during each of her shifts. Most of the pies were made from fresh fruit that was either grown with the vegetables or purchased from local farmers. Tully Milders said that it was during his study of this part of his family history that he became motivated to commit to a similar farm-to-table concept in future restaurant ventures of his own.

In a 1979 article in the *Fairfield Sun*, Mable Kohler Holbrock wrote that Mom Milders was kind in addition to being particular, and she insisted that all customers be served with generous portions of everything on her

MENU

COCKTAILS
[illegible]
Fresh Shrimp
Crab Meat
Oyster
Fruit

CHEESE
American
Roquefort
Swiss
Cream

SALADS
SOUR CREAM SLAW
Lettuce
Lettuce and Tomato
Combination
Asparagus Tips
Fruit
Chicken
Cucumber
Shrimp
Cottage Cheese

OMELETTES
Plain
Spanish
Jelly
Ham
Onion

VEGETABLES
Fresh in Season
FRENCH FRIED ONIONS
POTATOES

DINNER
FRESH SPRING CHICKEN
FROM THE CHARCOAL BURNER—PREMIUM SIRLOIN STRIP STEAKS $1.50 PER PERSON
SPECIAL FRIED CHICKEN SANDWICH $1.00
SPECIAL STEAK SANDWICH.......... 1.25
Our dinners are all freshly prepared—Reservations in advance enable us to give you better service.
"OPEN THE YEAR ROUND"

MILDERS FAMOUS HOME CANNED CORN
HOMEMADE CHICKEN BROTH NOODLES

COFFEE—TEA, ETC.
Postum
Milk
Coffee
Chocolate
Tea

DESSERTS
Pie
Ice Cream
Cake

SANDWICHES
ROAST CHICKEN
Ham
Beef
Cheese
Ham and Cheese
Ham and Tomato
Lettuce and Egg
Bacon
Bacon and Tomato
Grilled Cheese
Egg
Fried Ham

SPECIALS
Bacon and Eggs
Ham and Eggs
CLUB SANDWICH

SOUPS
Mock Turtle
Chili
Tomato
Noodle
Vegetable
Cream of Mushroom
Onion

Wines, Liquors and Mixed Drinks

BOTTLED IN BOND
Old Grandad
Old Taylor
Old Jordan
Kentucky Tavern
Seagram's V. O.
Old Overholt–Rye
Canadian Club

SCOTCH WHISKEY
Johnnie Walker (Black Label)
Catty Sark
White Horse
Black and White
Vat 69
Ballantine's
Old Angus

RUM
Bacardi (Yellow Label)
Ron Rico
Carioca

BRANDY
Hennessy XXX
Martel

FIZZES
Silver
Golden
Royal
New Orleans
Plain Gin

CORDIALS
Apricot Brandy
Benedictine–D. O. M.
Cherry Brandy
Creme de Menthe–(white)
Creme de Menthe–(green)
Curacao
Cointreau
Creme de Cocoa

SOURS
Whiskey
Gin
Brandy
Rum

HIGH BALLS
Scotch
Bourbon
Rye
Gin
Sloe Gin
Vermouth
Brandy

CHAMPAGNE
Mumm's
Renault

WHISKEYS
Bond and Lillard
Seagram–7
Four X
Four Roses
Boots and Saddle
Paul Jones
Crab Orchard
Cream of Kentucky
Old Jordan
5th Avenue
Old Republic

RICKEYS
Sloe Gin
Gin
Rum
Brandy

GIN
Fleischmann's
Gordon
Dekuyper–Sloe Gin

DRAUGHT BEER

BOTTLED BEER
Budweiser
Burger
Patrick Henry
Wiedemann's
Hudepohl
Brucks
Carling's Black Label

MIXED DRINKS
CHAMPAGNE COCKTAIL
Alexander Cocktail
Brandy, Creme de Cacao, Cream
Angel Tip
Maraschino, Creme de Cacao and Cream
Bacardi Cocktail
Rum, Lime Grenadine
Bronx Cocktail
Gin, Orange, Italian Vermouth
Clover Leaf Cocktail
Gin, Lime, White of Egg
Dry Martini
Gin, French Vermouth
Egg Nogg
Brandy, Rum, Egg, Sugar and Cream
Pink Lady
Gin, Lime Grenadine
Manhattan
Whiskey, Italian Vermouth, Bourbon
Martini
Gin, Italian and French Vermouth
Orange Blossom
Gin, Orange Flower and Juice
Old Fashion (Toddy)
Whiskey, Sugar, Lemon Peel, Fruit
Planter's Punch
Brandy, Port, Sugar, Lemon, Syphon, Fruit
Saratoga Sour
White of Egg, Whiskey, Lemon Juice, Sugar, Fruit
Side Car
Lemon Juice, Brandy and Cointreau
Stinger
Brandy and White Creme de Menthe
Tom Collins
Gin, Lime, Sugar, Imp. Soda
Reds Special
Apricot Liquer, French Vermouth, Orange Juice, Grenadine, Creme de Menthe
B. & B.
Benedictine and Brandy
Diaquari
Bacardi, Lime, Sugar
Dubonnet Cocktail
Dubonnet, Gin
The Thistle
Scotch, Bitters, Syrup and Italian Vermouth

The inside of the Milders Inn menu. *Tully Milders family photo.*

One of the German cooks at the Milders Inn in the 1920s. It's believed her last name was Armentrout. *Tully Milders family photo.*

menu, and calorie counting simply wasn't allowed. Likewise, holidays were extra special, with whole turkeys being baked and sliced on Thanksgiving and Christmas and placed on the tables as guests arrived. Waitresses then served additional delicious side dishes to enhance the joy of the festivities, again illustrating that the Milderses remained "nice people" in spite of their success. In another demonstration of Mom Milders's kindness, Tully Milders recently recounted a story that showed just how far his family would go to help those in need:

> *The story goes that in the first years at the inn, Jake and Mom raised their own chickens before they decided to buy them from local farmers. An alcoholic who lived nearby would sneak in their back field and steal the chickens and would then walk into the front of the inn and try to sell the same chickens back to Mom for a fee. Though Mom knew the man had stolen the chickens from her, she felt sorry for him and actually paid him the fee he asked, buying back her own chickens to serve to the inn's many guests.*

Tully said that in addition to the great food and great service at the inn, there was always liquor available in the bar, which was closed off from the main dining room. For those who chose to imbibe, a prime draft beer could be purchased for a nickel, and whiskey was always readily available. Tully said he often wondered if that was because of a family connection to the bootleg liquor trade. Though it was never proven, the fact remained that

The bar area inside the Milders Inn. *Tully Milders family photo.*

Above, left to right: Jake Milders, Ray Milders, Mary "Mom" Milders and Helen Milders, circa 1901. *Tully Milders family photo.*

Left: Mom and Jake Milders in the early twentieth century. *Tully Milders family photo.*

Jake and Mom Milders continued to sell alcohol throughout Prohibition, and with diners having to wait three hours to eat, readily available alcohol proved to be a popular asset. However, though whiskey was popular, it was always the food that was the main reason for the Milderses' success, and that became especially evident by Mom Milders's expanding waistline as she tasted her own cooking. Tully said that in 1901, before her son Ray was born, Mom Milders weighed less than one hundred pounds. However, after years of cooking and tasting to make sure her food was suitable for her clientele, Mom's weight topped out at over three hundred pounds, making it clear that, just as she didn't allow her customers to count calories, she also never counted them herself.

Ultimately, as Mom Milders's waistline grew, so did the scope of the Milders Inn customer base, and folks started coming to the inn from across the eastern United States. As a result, the peak of the Milderses' early success came right around the same time as Prohibition began in America. As the bootleg whiskey trade, crime and gambling grew in nearby Hamilton—a favorite hideout for many of the gangsters who defined the era—many well-known criminals also started finding their way to the restaurant, where they enjoyed the desolate location, the whiskey and the delicious food that made the Milders Inn great.

Chapter 3

PROHIBITION

Prohibition, or the prohibited sale of alcoholic beverages, began in the United States on January 16, 1919, with the ratification of the Eighteenth Amendment to the Constitution and the Volstead Act that enforced it. Likewise, on January 17, 1920, the Prohibition Amendment took effect, and across parts of the country, angry citizens and corrupt politicians ignored and defied the law, though there was strong initial support in the American South. As Prohibition arrived in America, it also arrived in Hamilton, the city that soon became known as "Little Chicago," which made a big impact on the Milders Inn, just a few miles to the south. Hamilton got the name Little Chicago because, during Prohibition, it became a haven for Chicago, Illinois–based gangsters who used to hide out here when they ran from the law. In his book *Little Chicago, A History of the Prohibition Era in Hamilton, and Butler County, Ohio*, historian Jim Blount wrote: "By the mid-1920's, Hamilton, Ohio—like Chicago, Illinois—was known for its bold and open defiance of prohibition and other laws and moral codes. One crusading minister said in 1925, that it 'is easier to buy moonshine than milk,' in Hamilton."

Blount said Prohibition wasn't popular at all in the city, where at least sixty-nine saloons operated and were suddenly forced to close. Likewise, four days after its start, the Butler County commissioners raised property taxes 8.25 percent to compensate for the $26,000 lost by the abolishment of liquor taxes. Because of the devastating financial impact for Hamilton and Butler County, Blount said that there was an immediate backlash, and as a result, illegal liquor distribution became a way of life:

> *A Hamilton City Councilman and two former Hamilton saloonkeepers were arrested in January 1920 for violating federal prohibition laws. George J. Renners, a Hamilton councilman at large who also had been a saloon operator in East Hamilton, Dennis Buckley, a saloonkeeper in Hamilton before prohibition, and a third man with local connections were arrested and charged with being part of a complex liquor distribution scheme involving distillers, businessmen, government agents and police in Cincinnati, Louisville, Chicago and New York City.*

Just as Hamilton was known as an American industrial giant in the late nineteenth and early twentieth centuries, the city and surrounding areas were now known for their connection to organized crime. Though there was no proven connection between the Milderses and the illegal liquor trade, the above example proves that bootlegging infiltrated the top levels of local society, and everyone was suspect as far as their possible involvement. As the business of illegal liquor distribution grew, so did the violence that surrounded the trade, and Hamilton- and Butler County–area police simply weren't able to stop the gangs who took over the area. Bank robberies, murders and hijackings were rampant, and notorious criminals like John Dillinger and Bob Zwick were regularly spotted around town—and eventually, they became part of the scenery at the Milders Inn.

JOHN DILLINGER

The food, the service and the commitment to discretion made the Milders Inn a desirable place for gangsters like John Dillinger, but in spite of his reputation as a killer, on at least one occasion, Mom Milders was quick to show Dillinger who was in charge at her restaurant:

> *The story goes that one night John Dillinger came into the inn wearing a black fedora. Mom was a stickler about men not wearing hats when they ate at the inn, and it upset her that he did not remove his fedora when he sat down. Mom, who was six feet tall and over three hundred pounds by this point, reportedly went up to Dillinger and said: "I know who you are, and you are more than welcome to eat here. But we do not allow men to wear hats, and if you plan to stay, you will need to remove your hat before you are served."*

Tully Milders, who told this story, said Dillinger reportedly never said a word to Mom after her demand, but he did take off his fedora and place it on his knee while he finished his meal. Though many of her friends weren't surprised that Mom Milders had the courage to stand up to John Dillinger, one look at the criminal's background shows that Dillinger was not a man to be messed with.

According to his FBI dossier, Dillinger was born on June 22, 1903, in Oak Hill, an Indianapolis suburb. His background was nothing like the loving Milders family, as he was raised in an atmosphere of extremes by a father who often disciplined him harshly but then became generous and permissive when the mood suited him. Dillinger's mother died when he was three, and after his father remarried, he grew resentful of his stepmother, which led to teenage years filled with anger and trouble. After dropping out of school, Dillinger moved from job to job, eventually joining the navy, which he promptly deserted when his ship docked in Boston. By 1924, Dillinger, a twenty-one-year-old malcontent, had returned home to Indiana and married Beryl Hovius, who was just sixteen years old when she became the wife of America's future most wanted.

By the time 1933 rolled around, John Dillinger had been sentenced to two consecutive prison terms after he and his gang terrorized the Midwest. After his parole, Dillinger eventually ended up in the Hamilton area, where he learned about the Milders Inn and its reputation for being a great place to drink and dine. Though his gang arrived at their Second Street hideout first, after a post-parole crime spree that left Dillinger in jail in Lima, they eventually broke him out, killing Sheriff Jess L. Sarber in the process. As a nationwide manhunt ensued, Dillinger remained in Hamilton for several months, and it was on at least one occasion that he visited the Milders Inn and the above incident occurred.

BOB ZWICK

In addition to Dillinger's visit, other noted gangsters like Bob Zwick and Hamilton's own Joseph "Turkey Joe" Jacobs regularly dined at the Milders Inn, and Zwick's girlfriend, Dago Rose Meyer, worked there as a waitress. Known as "The Fox," Bob Zwick was one of the most feared and best known of the criminals who operated out of Hamilton/Little Chicago in the late 1920s and early 1930s. Likewise, Dago Rose Meyer played an integral part in many of the stories surrounding his legacy. In fact, one of the most widely known stories about Zwick came when it was falsely reported that he died in a crime spree that included a bank robbery at the Butler County Somerville Bank in 1930. Somerville, a small village located on the Preble County border, was another area that was heavily populated by German immigrants and was about thirty miles north of the Milders Inn. The Somerville Bank was near the general store, and this writer's grandmother worked there and waited on Bob Zwick just hours before the robbery occurred. Just twenty-nine years old at the time, Nellie Withrow Hoel said that Zwick was very polite when he visited her on that fateful day, proving that some of America's most notorious criminals could be quite personable if they had to deal with local citizens whom they didn't want to get in their way. Meanwhile, the reports about Zwick's death after the robbery came about because three of his gang members were captured shortly afterward, and many thought that Zwick's not being captured meant that he had died in the confusion. Even Jake and Mom Milders, who seemed to have a close relationship with Zwick, weren't certain that he had survived.

Likewise, a second incident in early 1932, this time involving Milders Inn waitress Dago Rose Meyer, once again had the locals thinking that Zwick was dead. On March 5 of that year, two women were killed out of the area, near Balsam Lake, Wisconsin, after being shot to death while riding in a car. It was believed that the women knew too much about gang activity in that area and others, and after the shooting, one of the victims was identified as "Irish Rose," who was supposedly from Hamilton, Ohio. While sitting at the bar at the Milders Inn, the customers began to speculate that "Irish Rose" was actually Dago Rose Meyer because she hadn't been seen at work. Apparently, there were also similarities in the descriptions of the two women, and like "Irish Rose," Dago Rose Meyer claimed she arrived in Hamilton to wait tables after working in her home state of New York. Because many believed that Meyer died in the shooting, they felt that it proved that Bob Zwick was also dead because of the deep connection the Milders Inn waitress had to his criminal activities.

Though stories about the pair's death continued to circulate in the following years, Bob Zwick and Dago Rose Meyer were both alive and well, and Meyer still worked for the Milderses when she wasn't in jail or engaged in criminal activities of her own. Though no one ever accused Meyer of being the connection between the Milderses and bootleg whiskey—and it's still not known if she was—the waitress finally ended up in jail for her connection to Zwick. In spite of all the rumors and false reports, Bob Zwick actually outlived his girlfriend, the Milderses and all of his gang members, dying of old age in a Cincinnati nursing home in 1997, just three months shy of his 100th birthday.

TURKEY JOE JACOBS

Meanwhile, Joseph "Turkey Joe" Jacobs, another regular customer at the Milders Inn, was not as fortunate as Bob Zwick, having died in the 1929 ambush (mentioned in the prologue of this book) that occurred nearby. Though there are several different versions to the story, Hamilton native and local butcher Vernon Horning told the *Cincinnati Enquirer* in 1999 that he remembered being a young boy at the time and said he watched folks line up on Nilles Road to view Jacobs's body after he was shot to death. "I'll never forget seeing an [police] officer sticking a finger in the dead guy's bullet hole, [and] it was Turkey Joe Jacobs, shot in the head. A woman fainted on the spot," said Horning.

After the murder, the May 28, 1929 headline of the *Hamilton Evening Journal* read, "Bullet Riddled Body of Jacobs Found as Pal (Zwick) Escapes with Life." The paper reported that the thirty-eight-year-old Jacobs, though officially a Hamilton businessman, was an alleged beer and whiskey runner and strong-arm henchman for at least one bootleg gang. Over the years, many have speculated that he, and not Dago Rose Meyer, might have been the actual connection between the Milderses and their whiskey, but again, no one knows for sure. Jacobs reportedly got the nickname "Turkey Joe" because of his official title as a stock trader. However, legend also has it that the nickname was given to Jacobs by fellow gangsters after he attempted to rob what he thought was a liquor truck but was actually a farmer's truck filled with turkeys that proceeded to attack him as he broke in. Shortly after his murder, the *Journal* reported a complicated story involving Jacobs's family, saying that his wife said he told her he was headed to a greenhouse on River Road in Fairfield on the night of his death. He supposedly wanted to pick out flowers for the upcoming Decoration (Memorial) Day holiday. She claimed not to have known that he was meeting Bob Zwick at the Milders Inn to plan what was believed to be another liquor heist. Likewise, Jacobs's mother said that her son was merely a victim of mistaken identity in the shooting, and she insisted that he was not a gangster as had been reported. In fact, she claimed that he was a decent man who loved children and always made sure that his own kids had nice clothes and good food to eat. However, in spite of her declarations of her son's innocence, when she was asked to provide a picture of him for the newspaper, Jacobs's mother said that he never allowed his photograph to be taken and added that, to her knowledge, none existed. Even with the vast number of photos in the Milderses' and other local historical collections, no picture of Turkey Joe Jacobs has ever been found.

Though the circumstances surrounding Jacobs's death still remain a mystery, the impact it had on the Milders Inn was profound. In the prologue of this book, Tully Milders said that Mom Milders hid Bob Zwick under her skirt after the nearby ambush that killed Jacobs, but the *Hamilton Daily News* reported yet another detailed story. In the May 28, 1929 edition, that paper said that Blanche Hoffman (the driver of the car that Bob Zwick hijacked after he was shot) claimed she heard Zwick cry out to Mom Milders after she took him to the inn and helped him into the dining room. "Hide me quick, Mary! They are after me!" Hoffman said that Zwick yelled, running to hide behind Mom Milders as she ran out of the kitchen to see what was wrong.

The paper said that the "they" Zwick was referring to was the brown sedan full of gangsters who had killed Turkey Joe Jacobs. Hoffman told the paper that as Zwick hid behind Mom Milders, the car full of killers approached the inn, and to prevent a shootout inside, Zwick reportedly ran to the middle of the road outside and tried to hail several cars to take him from the area. Zwick was reportedly bleeding profusely and was on the verge of collapse, but Hoffman said he held a pistol and threatened everyone who drove by. She said when no one picked him up, he ran about two hundred feet north of the Milders Inn to a store owned by Phillip Beiser and tried to get inside to hide. However, knowing who he was, Beiser's wife refused to let the gangster in and slammed the door in his face, locking him out. After this, Zwick supposedly ran back to the road and hijacked a car driven by a man identified by police as "Mr. Blair" and forced the man to take him to Turkey Joe Jacobs's house on Jersey Avenue in Hamilton, where Jacobs's Buick Sedan was still parked out front. Zwick, a woman believed to be his girlfriend and Milders Inn waitress Dago Rose Meyer supposedly got in the car in this version of the story and forced Mr. Blair to drive them to a home on Welch Avenue. Though Hoffman never told the paper how Dago Rose Meyer ended up with her gangster boyfriend after he left the inn, the newspaper reported that she was with him at Jacobs's house and said that after they arrived, Meyer gave Mr. Blair five dollars and told him he would not be needed anymore. The next day, the paper said that police caught up with Mr. Blair and made him drive the route that Zwick had forced him to cover the night before. Ultimately, they ended up back at the Welch Avenue house, which was owned by a man named Evans, who had reportedly been friends with Turkey Joe Jacobs. However, by the time the police returned to Evans's home, Bob Zwick and Dago Rose Meyer had escaped, and Turkey Joe Jacobs's killers were never found.

In a third story about that fateful night, Ray Milders told *Fairfield Sun* contributor Mable Kohler Holbrock in 1980 that after the murder of Turkey Joe Jacobs, a man believed to be Bob Zwick came to the inn and yelled at his mother to hide him from the killers who were hot on his trail: "Mom said, 'See that little shed in the backyard? You go back there, go inside and you can lock the door from the inside and no one will know you are there.' Mom said he followed instructions, and she sent him back there because she did not want a hysterical man with a gun in her kitchen."

In his account of the story, Ray Milders said Dago Rose Meyer was not working the night of the shooting and that Zwick left the inn and forced a Fairfield man with the last name of "Hunger" to drive him to her house. Milders, like others, said Dago Rose Meyer was a well-known underworld figure at the time, in addition to being Zwick's girlfriend and his mother's waitress. He said his mother remained "very cool and collected" throughout the whole incident.

While the true story lies somewhere in the middle of the three accounts of the ambush, the impact of the incident is still being felt in this area today. The *Hamilton Journal News* once again recounted the story in 2013, when Tully Milders first decided to host Milders Inn night at Ryan's Tavern, where he currently works. Likewise, Milders said that throughout the Prohibition years, many other noted gangsters of Little Chicago fame ate at the Milders Inn, though not much is known about them. However, as historian Jim Blount told the *Cincinnati Enquirer* in 1999, it was believed that the nearby Stockton Club, another local speakeasy located at Seward Road and Dixie Highway, was controlled by a Detroit group known as the Purple Gang, a group closely allied with noted gangster Al Capone. As such, it is very likely that the Milders Inn hosted Capone and perhaps many more of the gangsters who defined the era. But in spite of all the turmoil and infamous guests, the Milderses never sacrificed the quality of their food or their top-notch customer service to their everyday clientele. Even though many would describe some of their guests as "thugs," the Prohibition years actually enhanced the reputation of the Milders Inn, and it was still considered one of the finest restaurants in the country. Perhaps that's because Jake and Mom did not fall victim to the lower-class barfights that had plagued H.J. Meyers at the restaurant so many years before.

Shortly after Prohibition ended and the gangsters moved on, the Milderses' son, Ray, took over the restaurant as his parents were nearing retirement age. As Ray arrived, so did another era at the inn, this time with entertainment being part of the day-to-day operations. Where Jake Milders was known around Hamilton and Fairfield Township for his strong business acumen and popular restaurant, Ray Milders had national connections to the world of music, and as a result, more fame, fortune and celebrity soon found their home at the Milders Inn.

Part II
The Transition

Chapter 4

RAY

The Early Years

On May 2, 1901, Mom Milders gave birth to her only son, Ray, who would later take over as the owner and general manager of the Milders Inn. As a boy, Ray attended Harrison School in Hamilton, and like his father and grandfather, he had many interests and talents, including Jake Milders's love for sports and music. By the time he reached Hamilton High School, Ray was an outstanding basketball and baseball player, having first received exposure to America's favorite pastime when he served as the batboy for his father's Krebs baseball team. (Though the Milderses still lived in Fairfield Township above the Milders Inn, the Hamilton School District was the one that served the area.) After his high school graduation in 1919, Ray went on to Miami University in Oxford, where he became the star pitcher for the university baseball team. A 1921 article in the *Cincinnati Enquirer* reported that Ray was an outstanding athlete at Miami who was eventually scouted for professional play by the Cleveland Indians, as well as the former St. Louis Nationals. In 1922, Ray was also named to the All-Ohio Basketball Team, representing the school.

After graduating from Miami in 1923, Ray met and married Margaret (Lail) Milders on November 28, 1925, in Marion County, Indiana. Margaret, born in 1906 in Colorado, came to Indiana to attend college and met Ray after he became a singer while still playing sports at Miami. As a newlywed couple, they first lived across the street from the Milders Inn, until their new home—the first one built in the nearby neighborhood of Ziliox Woods (now called Shady Lane)—was finished. In 1930, the house was valued at

$9,000. The Milderses added tennis and volleyball courts, a shooting range and floodlights to their new backyard, an addition that would prove to be very important to them in the years to come. Though World War II caused property values to drop, the house is worth $97,000 today, but at just one and a half stories tall, it is hard to imagine more than two or three people living there. But household needs weren't as great in Ray Milders's generation, and while living in Ziliox Woods, Ray and Margaret had three children: Maryland, known as "Petie," born in 1927 and the woman responsible for keeping the stories of the Milders Inn alive; William Milders, later an accountant and Tully Milders's father, born in 1933; and Robert Milders, born in 1948, whose varied past includes stints as a nuclear physicist, a Vietnam soldier and the head of a motorcycle club in Wyoming, where he still lives. According to the 1930 census, the Milderses also took in a Russian couple as boarders in the early years of their marriage: Harry Leshner, an iron worker, and his wife, Ethel, a nurse. Later, in 1940, the Milderses hired a live-in maid, eighteen-year-old Emma Bacher, a clear indication that business was booming when Ray took over at the Milders Inn.

But that all came later. First, as a star athlete, a gifted singer and an eventual businessman, Ray Milders's life resembled that of his grandfather Peter and his father, Jake. He, too, was happy and successful, and he, too, had a

Ray and Margaret Milders's Fairfield, Ohio home as it looks today. *Captured Beauty Photography.*

Left to right: William Milders, Marilyn "Petie" Milders, Mary "Mom" Milders, Ray Milders and Mom Milders's mother, Marilyn Heet Dollman (seated), in the late 1930s. *Tully Milders family photo.*

commitment to friends and family. In spite of his early success in playing sports, it was ultimately music that captured Ray's heart, and his decision to follow a career path of singing earned him his wife and eventually brought entertainment to the Milders Inn. In a 1981 article in the *Hamilton Journal News*, Margaret Milders remembered when she first met her husband, and she said it was Ray's beautiful baritone singing voice and handsome features that attracted her to him. Likewise, she said his vocal abilities led him to tour with many bands across Ohio and Indiana. Margaret said Ray's vocal skills eventually earned him a scholarship to Cincinnati's Conservatory of Music while he was still a student in Oxford, and she said that it was also during these years that he began to make friends with many influential musicians: "Ray knew Hoagy Carmichael from Lake Manatau, Indiana (where they both played), and one night while he was still at Miami, Hoagy called him and told him to get a flatbed truck and a piano and they would go on a serenade for the girls at the school. Hoagy also used to serenade the girls at Indiana University, where I was."

In his 1965 autobiography, *Sometimes I Wonder*, Carmichael recounted Margaret Milders's story in even greater detail:

> *Oxford, Ohio was a pretty town, and CY* [Hoagie's nickname for Ray because he made the girls "sigh" with his voice and good looks] *Milders was a student there who was known as the "Campus Crooner." He was waiting for me* [after we agreed to meet] *in a truck with a piano ready to go. Girls' dormitories fairly covered the place and the game was to visit all of them with* [our] *truck and band. Batty* [Batty De Marcus, who played around Oxford with Ray Milders] *was in great form and CY's voice rang out* [that night] *like a bell full of gold coins.*

As Ray Milders developed the singing career that would help him keep the Milders Inn relevant in the years to come, it was his connection to the following famous musicians that made him a local celebrity who is still admired and talked about today.

HOAGY CARMICHAEL

Howard Hoagland Carmichael, known as "Hoagy," was born on November 22, 1899, in Bloomington, Indiana. In 1927, a few years after he met Ray Milders, his career as a composer, singer, actor and bandleader began when he wrote the American classic "Stardust." Later on, it was Carmichael who also wrote "Georgia on My Mind," made famous in 1960 by singer Ray Charles. He also arranged and recorded the hit "Up a Lazy River," which was written by Sidney Arodin. In addition to his recording career, Carmichael was an actor who appeared in fourteen movies, winning his first Academy Award in 1951 for co-writing the song "In the Cool, Cool, Cool of the Evening" with his good friend the equally famous Johnny Mercer. Throughout his career, Hoagy Carmichael remained friends with Ray Milders.

As Carmichael went on to fame and fortune in Hollywood, Ray Milders also took to the road after college, joining the Charlie Davis Orchestra in Indianapolis. Formed in Indiana in the late 1920s, the group had a major impact on the swing jazz movement that was emerging in America, and in addition to Ray Milders, its lead vocalist was Dick Powell, who later left music for acting. It was Powell who was the first to play Detective Phillip Marlowe on screen. These affiliations with Hoagy Carmichael, Dick Powell and Charlie Davis created a connection between Ray Milders and many other famous actors and actresses, such as Powell's two wives, Joan Blondell and June Allyson.

BIX BEIDERBECKE

Ray Milders's work with Hoagy Carmichael also led him to form a short-term musical relationship with one of America's top jazz performers of the 1920s. Bix Beiderbecke, along with Louis Armstrong, brought the genre to popularity, and in a 1974 book about his life, *Bix, Man & Legend*, author Richard M. Sudhalter recounted the first time Beiderbecke heard Ray Milders sing his famous song, "I'll See You in My Dreams." The two met that night in the rooftop garden of Indianapolis's Severin Hotel. With both Beiderbecke and Carmichael in the audience, Ray Milders wowed them with his rendition of the song, and Beiderbecke was very impressed with Ray's ability to woo the women in the audience. The book also mentioned the close relationship Bix Beiderbecke had with Hamilton pianist Dud Mecum, a name that would later be very important to Ray Milders and his family, as Beiderbecke and Mecum worked for a short time together at Fairfield's Stockton Club. Sadly, the days of performing in bars took their toll on Beiderbecke, who was a serious alcoholic. After leaving the Stockton Club and heading back out on the road, he died shortly after winning a Grammy for his recording of Hoagy Carmichael's "Georgia on My Mind." He was just twenty-eight years old. Though the official cause of death was listed as pneumonia, the mysterious circumstances surrounding Beiderbecke's demise have left historians stumped for decades as to what actually killed him, adding even greater interest to the overall story about the Milders family. Later in 1954, Louis Armstrong paid tribute to his young friend Beiderbecke, saying that he was the kind of musician who would make folks stand up just at the mention of his name. Likewise, he was the kind of musician who, because of his talent and celebrity, had a very close relationship with Ray Milders.

Meanwhile, though Ray Milders spent a lot of time on the road rubbing elbows with the rich and famous, he decided to give up that life in the early 1930s and settled into his role as the head of his family. It was during this time that he ended up working at the Milders Inn with his parents, Jake and Mom. Ray never forgot his connections, though, and eventually brought top-notch musical entertainment to the restaurant, where he also wowed audiences with his own singing. Though by this point, the Great Depression had taken its toll on the inn, the addition of live music began to once again turn things around, and life for the Milders family returned to its previous successful state for a short time. That is, until once again tragedy struck them in early 1935. On January 3 of that year, Ray's father, Jake, was recovering from a year of poor health when he suddenly had a massive heart attack and went into a coma. Three days later, on Sunday, January 6, Jacob Milders died, leaving his only son, Ray, to take over his legacy as a businessman and as a family man and friend. As Ray contemplated filling the shoes of his father, newspapers from around the region paid tribute to the man who by this point was known simply as Jake:

> *Known across the Midwest for his part in the development of baseball, he was known as a sportsman throughout this section of the country for the part he played in developing the sport. He is remembered too in Hamilton as the owner of the Coliseum on North B Street that was swept away in the 1913 flood, and Milders' Inn has been a landmark on the Mount Pleasant Pike for many years.*
>
> —Cincinnati Enquirer, *Jake Milders's obituary, January 6, 1935*

> *Perhaps no man was better known in Hamilton and vicinity than Jacob Milders…In every undertaking Mr. Milders was efficient and* [he] *always kept in mind that service to the public was the chief element of* [his] *success, aside from furnishing the best of entertainment along his particular lines of endeavor.* [He was] *of an unusually kindly nature, never given to unseemly gossip about anyone, helpful in every way possible,* [and] *he had a host of loyal friends who will deeply regret to learn of his death.*
>
> —Hamilton Journal, *Jake Milders's obituary, January 8, 1935*

The several-page obituary that appeared in the *Hamilton Journal* recounted the life of Jake Milders in great detail, and mourners came from around the region to pay their respects to the much-loved man.

After Jake's passing and burial in Hamilton's Rose Hill Cemetery, Mom Milders continued to work in the kitchen at the Milders Inn, though she, too, was nearing retirement age. In mid-1935, Ray Milders completely remodeled the inn to make it more suitable for the musical performances he began. With Ray's music already being responsible for bringing in thousands of customers during the short time he worked at the inn, his greatest success came when he became partners with Bix Beiderbecke's old friend, the well-known Hamilton pianist Dud Mecum. Mecum, like Ray Milders, had many famous musical friends, and he was also the co-writer of one of America's all-time favorite dance songs, the 1925 hit "Angry."

DUD MECUM

Born in Hamilton in 1896, Dudley "Dud" Mecum was stricken with typhoid fever after the 1913 flood, and after graduating from Hamilton High School in 1914, he was sent by doctors to Spokane, Washington, where it was believed his health would improve. After spending time there, Mecum's health did improve, and he joined the National Guard and was then transferred to Mexico before returning back to Washington State to study mining and engineering. Mecum was musically inclined, and while he was in college, he played piano at frat houses to pay his rent. After graduation, he joined the U.S. Navy and continued to play piano across America and Europe before being discharged in 1919. Following his discharge, Dud Mecum returned to Washington and then went to Chicago to pursue a career in writing and worked for several publishing houses there. In a 1965 article in the *Hamilton Journal News*, Mecum told writer Jim Newton that one of his biggest breaks came when he met Irving Berlin, who recognized his talents as a composer and pianist. He said he was playing at Chicago's Silver Slipper club when, during a dance intermission, Berlin came over and sat down at his piano bench: "He said he had two songs, yet unpublished that he was not sure about. Berlin asked me if I would play them and offer my candid opinion about them. [Afterward] I said, 'Mr. Berlin, I'd give my right arm to have written either one of them.'"

As a result of Mecum's praise, Irving Berlin published the two songs, which became the American favorites "Say It Isn't So" and "How Deep Is the Ocean," two tunes that were reportedly played by Mecum and sung by Ray Milders in later years at the inn.

The front page of the Milders Inn menu with Dud Mecum and Ray Milders pictured. *Tully Milders family photo.*

After his time in Chicago, Dud Mecum decided to return home to Hamilton in the late 1920s, and upon arrival, he formed a band and began playing piano with Bix Beiderbecke at Fairfield's Stockton Club, where he wrote the song "It's Always Raining" for Ray Milders's friend Dick Powell, who sang it in the 1933 movie *Broadway through a Keyhole*. It wasn't much later that Beiderbecke left the club, and Mecum decided to make yet another move, though this time he stayed close by and became the pianist at the

Milders Inn. With Mecum on piano and Ray Milders on vocals, the two provided thousands of hours of dining and dancing for the crowds who still made the inn their favorite stop.

Ray Milders told *Fairfield Sun* writer Mable Kohler Holbrock in 1979 that he would go table to table singing to the guests at the inn as Mecum played piano. Saying their repertoire was made up of "sweet songs and not jazz," Milders credited Mecum with helping the Milders Inn stay successful through difficult financial times. Holbrock wrote, "Dudley was a well-known musician at that time, being a composer of many popular pieces. He composed a lot of parities to the popular songs of those days and we sang them night after night for the patrons of the [Milders] inn, who loved them. One of Dudley's hit songs "Angry" [written in 1925], is still popular today [in 1979]."

Later, noted Hamilton businessman and author Bill Rentschler wrote a letter to Ray Milders's daughter, Petie, in 2002, sharing his memories of spending time at the inn when he was a boy: "I remember so well those family dinners between the ages of about 6 or 7 until I turned about 17. I

Ray Milders and Dud Mecum, circa late 1930s. *Tully Milders family photo.*

have fond memories and a vivid picture of Ray Milders, tall and gracious and rather stately. He always went out of his way to be friendly and kindly to us kids, and he called me Billy."

In addition to their work at the Milders Inn, Ray Milders and Dud Mecum were regularly heard on WCKY radio in Greater Cincinnati. Founded by longtime Cincinnati broadcaster L.B. Wilson, WCKY went on the air in 1929, as Milders and Mecum became popular musicians. Due to its being licensed in Covington, Kentucky, the FCC allowed WCKY to increase power to fifty thousand watts in 1939, even though it was literally across the river from fifty-thousand-watt giant WLW. As such, the musical talents of Ray Milders and Dud Mecum were eventually heard from coast to coast, and in spite of their individual popularity, Milders and Mecum continued to work together at the Milders Inn until it closed in 1942.

Chapter 5

THE CINCINNATI REDS

With Ray Milders back at home, married with children and living nearby, life was pleasant for his family. His daughter, Petie, and his son William helped out around the Milders Inn as kids, and by the time Petie was a teenager in 1940, her dad was still singing, Dud Mecum was still playing piano and—in yet another strange twist for the Milders Inn—members of the Cincinnati Reds baseball team began hanging out there. Petie said that she and her family formed a bond with the Reds players that remained throughout all their lives. Petie, who later became Petie Milders Murphy, told *Hamilton Journal News* columnist Ercel Eaton in 1995 that though her family's involvement with the Reds players brought both joy and sorrow, some of her closest friends were the superstars who made up the team's roster:

> *The Reds won the pennant in 1940 and* [one of their star players] *Harry Craft got married in our living room on Shady Lane that same year. It was one of those hot summers and a lot of the team members would come out to eat at the inn, and would end up spending the night on the patio of my parents' house which was close by. Shady Lane was known as Ziliox Woods then, and ours was the first house in the neighborhood, with the rest of the area being country. Frank McCormick was also married at our home that year, and both McCormick and Craft were my favorite players. I was a member of both wedding parties.*

Ray and Margaret Milders's Fairfield, Ohio patio, where the members of the Cincinnati Reds slept on the hot summer nights of 1938, '39 and '40. *Captured Beauty Photography.*

Reds first baseman Frank McCormick shooting clay pigeons with Ray Milders, circa 1940. *Tully Milders family photo.*

Tully Milders said his aunt Petie and his grandfather Ray always told him stories about the Reds players who spent their weekends at the family home:

> *I was always told that the Reds wanted to get away from their fans when they partied after the games. With the trolley stopping right outside the Milders Inn, they could come there and no one would bother them. Likewise, many of the players would head over to my grandparents' house, where they could shoot clay pigeons, play basketball and continue partying. My grandmother would let them sleep outside, and then they would go back*

New Year's Eve, circa 1937 or 1938, at the Milders Inn. *Left to right*: Ray Milders, Powell Crosley, Gwendolyn Crosley and Mom Milders. *Tully Milders family photo.*

> *to the inn the next morning, catch the trolley and go back to Cincinnati in time for the day's ballgame.*

Though Tully said the Reds players would shoot the clay pigeons in his grandparents' backyard, his aunt Petie said she would also go with them to nearby fields to shoot. In addition to Harry Craft and Frank McCormick, other notable players who regularly visited the inn and Ray Milders's family home were Ernie Lombardi, Lew Riggs, Bill Myers, Ival Goodman, Bucky Walters, Joe Beggs, Gene Thompson, announcer Waite Hoyt, Dick Bray and Willard Hershberger. Likewise, Reds owner Powell Crosley was often spotted at the inn, even ringing in at least one New Year's there, as he enjoyed the music of Ray Milders and Dud Mecum. Tully said his grandfather Ray always told the story of Crosley sneaking out of the dining room to join Mom Milders in the kitchen, where he would nibble on cheese and crackers while he waited for her to finish his portion of her famous fried chicken. Though names like the above are familiar to both die-hard baseball fans and members of generations gone by, the importance of their dining at the Milders Inn cannot be fully understood today without taking a look back at each of their individual accomplishments.

POWELL CROSLEY

Powell Crosley Jr. was born on September 18, 1886, in Cincinnati. After completing his first year of high school in College Hill, the school closed, and he transferred to the Ohio Military Institute and then the University of Cincinnati. Crosley quit college after two years because of his obsession with the automobile and the way it worked. It was this obsession that led Crosley and his brother Lewis to form a company in 1907 in Connersville, Indiana, where they built an inexpensive automobile known as the Marathon Six. The car failed, and as a result, Crosley took a job with the Fisher Automobile Company in Indianapolis, but he was fired when he broke his arm trying to start a car. Still obsessed with automobile mechanics, Crosley next worked at numerous auto manufacturers in Indianapolis and Muncie, Indiana, and often told friends that he was supposed to be a starting driver in the Indianapolis 500 but he never got the chance because he couldn't find a sponsor.

Between 1910 and 1915, Crosley moved back to Cincinnati, got married and had two children. He continued to try to manufacture his own automobile and continued to fail before he found success in automobile accessories. In 1916, he co-founded the American Automobile Accessory Company with Ira J Cooper, and their bestseller was a tire reliner that was eventually bought by Sears. By 1919, he had generated over $1 million in auto accessory sales, and he began diversifying into other arenas, including the manufacture of phonograph cabinets.

In the early 1920s, Powell Crosley's son asked him for a radio, which was just becoming popular, and this request led Crosley to the career that made him one of the most famous people in American history. Crosley, shocked at the $100 price tag, instead bought his son a book called *The A.B.C. of Radio*, and the two built their own. Recognizing the appeal of the product, Crosley decided to bring the radio to the masses, and by 1924, he had formed the Crosley Radio Corporation, becoming the largest manufacturer of radios in the world. Once he became successful in radio manufacturing, he next decided to develop broadcasting so people would continue to buy his radios. As a result, he began experimenting with a twenty-watt transmitter that he built in his home, which led him to form the Crosley Broadcasting Corporation, which in turn led to him taking over at fifty-thousand-watt radio station WLW, across the river from where Ray Milders and Dud Mecum would later become stars. By the 1930s, Crosley had moved into the appliance business and was the first to come up with the concept of putting shelves on the doors of refrigerators. He also began manufacturing top-load washing machines when they came into being, and many of his appliance inventions are still being made by other companies today.

After all his success, Crosley bought the Cincinnati Reds baseball team in 1934 from owner Sidney Weil, who had been devastated by the stock market crash of 1929. He renamed the baseball park Crosley Field and secured permission from the baseball commissioner to hold seven night games there. Likewise, in another strange connection between Powell Crosley and the Milderses, Crosley began to understand the value of playing baseball at night, and on May 24, 1935, he was responsible for the the first night game in Major League Baseball history, which was held at Crosley Field between the Reds and the Philadelphia Phillies. Just like Hamilton's own Jake Milders, who held the first semi-pro night game at Krebs Park decades before, Crosley recognized that playing games in the evening would make baseball more available to those who had to work during the day. As such, the addition of lights increased the Reds attendance by 400 percent. During Crosley's tenure as the owner of the Reds, he not only implemented the first night game, but he also hosted two All-Star games in Cincinnati, was responsible for the huge opening day festivities that are still celebrated today and headed up some of the most memorable teams in Reds history, including the 1940 World Champions, whose roster included many of the players who often dined with him and the Milderses. In spite of his international success, Powell Crosley was simply a great friend as far as Ray Milders and his family were concerned. To them, he was simply known as "Powell."

As Crosley often referred to himself as the "man with many jobs," his original dream of creating his own automobile didn't come until 1939, at about the same time he befriended the Milderses. The Crosley Motors Automobile had an eighty-inch wheel base and a small two-cylinder air-cooled engine and was offered in gray, yellow or blue, with all models having red wheels and a black top. Crosley Motors Automobile had plants in Cincinnati; Richmond, Indiana; and Marion, Ohio, and, in all, produced 5,757 cars. Strangely, the end of Crosley Motors Automobile was very similar to the end of the Milders Inn. Both were forced to shut down in 1942 as a result of hard times brought about by World War II.

WAITE HOYT AND DICK BRAY

There are very few baseball fans in Cincinnati who don't remember the name Waite Hoyt. Hoyt, otherwise known as "Schoolboy," first signed a professional baseball contract with the New York Giants when he was still a fifteen-year-old student at Erasmus High School in Brooklyn, New York. After playing just one game for the Giants, Hoyt began a twenty-one-year career playing with seven teams. He made his name, however, as a pitcher for the New York Yankees, helping them win three World Series in the 1920s. Likewise, Hoyt was considered the star pitcher of the 1927 Yankees, often considered the best team in baseball history. He was teammates with the likes of Babe Ruth and Lou Gehrig and finished his career as a pitcher with a lifetime 3.59 ERA and a record of 237 wins and 182 losses. He retired from the game in 1938.

During his retirement, Waite Hoyt not only enjoyed life at the Milders Inn, but he also became a popular announcer for the Cincinnati Reds, where he spent the next twenty-four years doing play-by-play for the team. It was also during his years in the broadcast booth that Hoyt joined many of the young ballplayers at the inn, along with fellow Reds broadcaster Dick Bray. In fact, according to Ray Milders in a 1978 letter to historian Esther Benzing, it was Bray who first brought the Reds into his world:

> *In 1938, Dick Bray was the one who first brought the Reds ballplayers to the inn. My wife Marge and I were personal friends of about 20 of them* [as a result]. *We were especially close to* [Frank] *McCormick,* [Harry] *Craft,* [Lew] *Riggs, Buck Walters,* [Ival] *Goodman and Hershberger. McCormick and Craft were married at our home in Ziliox Woods and we held their reception at the Inn.*

By the time Dick Bray got into broadcasting for the Reds, he was already well known in the Cincinnati athletic community. Born in the Cincinnati suburb of Hyde Park in 1903, Bray was a three-sport star at Xavier University, excelling in baseball, tennis and basketball. By 1933, he developed an interest in radio and worked on air at WKRC, WSAI and WLW, and one of his most notable broadcasting accomplishments came when he created the program *Fans in the Stands*, in which he would walk through the aisles at Crosley Field selecting fans to interview. Ray Milders and his family were often in the stands for those games and Bray's popular show. Through his format, he would conduct the interviews live, on-air, and each fan who participated would receive a free loaf of bread. During the off-season, Bray would alter the show and interview fans in downtown Cincinnati, calling it *Fans on the Street.* After hosting his radio shows and assisting Waite Hoyt in the broadcast booth for many years, Bray retired from broadcasting in the 1960s and became the public relations director for a local glass company. He died in January 1986 and was preceded in death by Hall of Famer Hoyt, in August 1984. Again, though Waite Hoyt and Dick Bray were famous names throughout America in the mid-twentieth century, back home with the Milderses, they were just two more of the many celebrities whom Ray and Margaret called friends and who defined the clientele during the final years at the Milders Inn.

Though it was Dick Bray who first introduced many of the Reds to Ray and Margaret Milders, there was ultimately no one closer to the couple and their family than Harry Craft, Frank McCormick and Lew Riggs.

HARRY CRAFT

On August 5, 1995, the headline from Conroe, Texas, announced the death of former Cincinnati Reds outfielder Harry Craft. Shortly after his death, Petie Milders Murphy sat down with *Hamilton Journal News* columnist Ercel Eaton to share stories of the man who often ate at her family's restaurant and got married at her family's home:

> *One time I caught a baseball* [at the Reds game] *and Craft had all of the team members sign it. Likewise, in those days there was nothing but woods south of Nilles and only a few buildings around, and Craft was one of the ballplayers who would go with my dad to what is now Rolling Hills and shoot clay pigeons. I used to be allowed to go along.*

Petie said she last saw Harry Craft in 1988, when she was in the company of Sheldon Bender, a Reds official who lived in Hamilton and with whom she often attended games because he patronized the Milders Inn and befriended her family. They were at the ballpark one day when Bender heard that Craft was there, so he decided Petie Milders and Harry Craft should have a reunion, since they hadn't seen each other in decades. "'Harry took one look at me, put his arms around me and cried like a baby. That was the last time I ever saw him,' Petie said, as he died a short time later."

The baseball hit by Reds third baseman Lew Riggs that Harry Craft had the entire team sign for Marilyn "Petie" Milders, circa 1940. The brick is from the patio at Ray Milders's home, where the Reds partied during the summers of 1938 to 1940. *Tully Milders family photo.*

Harry Craft was born on April 19, 1915, in Ellisville, Mississippi. After attending Mississippi College in Clinton, he made his debut in the Major Leagues with the Reds on September 19, 1937, at the age of twenty-two. Known as "Wildfire," Craft played centerfield and had six good years with the Reds, his best coming in 1938, with fifteen home runs and eighty-three RBIs. He was also part of the pennant-winning Reds team in 1939 and the World Series–winning Reds team in 1940. Throughout these years, fans flocked to the Milders Inn just to catch a glimpse of Craft because of his success and popularity, and it was after the 1940 season that Harry Craft got married in Ray Milders's living room on what is now Shady Lane.

After leaving the Reds in 1942, with a lifetime batting average of .253, Craft went on and played for the minor-league team the Kansas City Blues until 1948. After his playing career ended, Craft became a manager in the New York Yankees system, managing Mickey Mantle during his first year in pro ball, and in 1955, he joined the Kansas City Athletics coaching staff and then replaced Lou Boudreau as that team's manager two years after that. In 1960, he moved to the Chicago Cubs franchise, and two years later, he moved to manage the expansion Houston Colt 45s and stayed there until

Reds centerfielder Harry Craft at Crosley Field, circa 1940. *Tully Milders family photo.*

Opposite: Reds centerfielder Harry Craft, 1940. *Tully Milders family photo.*

he was fired in 1964. From 1967 to 1991, Harry Craft remained a scout for several teams, including the Yankees, the Houston Astros and the San Francisco Giants. The seventy-six-year-old Craft finally retired from baseball just four years before he died, but throughout his post-playing career, he always returned to Cincinnati to revisit the team that had made him great and the friends like the Milderses whom he grew to love.

Author Bill Rentschler, in a 2002 letter to Petie Milders, said that Harry Craft and teammate Frank McCormick attended his mother's church, Trinity Episcopal, in Hamilton, and as a young boy, he said he got to know them at church and occasionally hang out with them at the Milders Inn:

> *Since I was a small boy, I loved baseball and the Reds. Mother's twin brother Mason Schlosser took me to my first ever game at Crosley Field and often thereafter since Dad was not a baseball fan. It was a special treat for me to come to the Milders Inn because of that, as there was always the prospect of seeing one or more of my heroes from the Reds. I kind of got to know Harry Craft and Frank McCormick and I saw them every so often at Milders.*

FRANK MCCORMICK

Frank McCormick was known as "Buck" for Frank Buck, a big game hunter and movie director, as McCormick loved to spend his free time shooting clay pigeons at and near the Milderses' home. Born on June 9, 1911, in New York City, McCormick played baseball as a young boy in sandlot, church league and high school, and by the age of seventeen, he had already decided to dedicate his life to the sport. After trying out and getting turned down for positions with the Philadelphia Athletics, Washington Senators and New York Giants, McCormick borrowed fifty dollars from his uncle in 1934 and traveled to Beckley, West Virginia, where he tried out for the Reds. Remembering that his sandlot manager had told him there would be more competition for outfield positions than first base, McCormick became a first baseman and was signed. At the end of the 1934 season, twenty-three-year-old Frank McCormick was called up to the big leagues and made his debut with Cincinnati on September 11 at Ebbets Field in Brooklyn, New York. After an unexciting first game, McCormick got two hits a few days later off Hall of Fame pitcher Carl Hubbell at the Polo Grounds, where he had failed at his tryout a few years before. Though McCormick hit .335 in his first stay with the Reds, he was sent back to the minors in 1935 before returning to the team in 1938 for good. After arriving back in the big leagues that year, McCormick, who stood six feet, four inches and weighed over two hundred pounds, was bigger than the average player of his day, and that led to him being third in batting in the entire National League.

Reds first baseman Frank McCormick shooting clay pigeons in the Milderses' backyard. *Tully Milders family photo.*

In 1940, when the Reds won the pennant, McCormick drove in 127 runs, led the league in hits and fielding and was voted the National League's Most Valuable Player. On October 8 of that year, Frank McCormick also married Vera Preedy in Ray Milders's backyard, and Petie Milders told the *Journal News* that it was very exciting for her to be a thirteen-year-old bridesmaid at the wedding, as all of her favorite Reds players who hung out at the Milders Inn were there.

Left to right: Reds players Harry Craft, Lew Riggs and Frank McCormick at Ray Milders's house on Frank McCormick's wedding day in 1938. *Tully Milders family photo.*

Though he had much success in the 1940 season, McCormick injured his back while swimming in a hotel pool, forcing him to be in a back brace for the rest of the season. This likely kept him out of military service in World War II, and his performance on the field began to decline. In 1945, as a result, the Reds sold McCormick to the Philadelphia Phillies, and though he continued to win recognition for his defensive playing, his batting average continued to drop. McCormick's last year in baseball came in 1948, when the Braves went to the World Series, and though he performed well, the thirty-seven-year-old was released by the Braves shortly after the season ended.

After his playing days were over, McCormick, like Harry Craft, remained in baseball as a manager, and in the mid-1950s, he returned to the Reds organization, this time as a television broadcaster. Frank McCormick died of cancer in Manhasset, New York, on November 21, 1982.

During his career as a player for the Reds, McCormick often stayed overnight at Ray and Margaret Milders's home, enjoying many picnics and parties. Petie Milders said in 2002 that McCormick was so close to her family that he actually called her parents "Ma" and "Pa." Shortly before McCormick died, his wife, Vera, wrote a letter to Fairfield historian Bob

Pendergrass, who up until recently owned Ray Milders's former Shady Lane home. Vera McCormick recalled the great times that she and her husband had in Fairfield:

> *We had such good times with the Milders* [sic] *and so many friends we made through them. Those were such wonderful years. We often try to visualize how our life would be different if we had stayed in Ohio. However, both our families were here in New York and it was a difficult decision to make. I understand the changes are so great there that we wouldn't even recognize the area. I shall always miss Ohio. There were so many good friends, happy days, and such wonderful memories.*

LEW RIGGS

Lew Riggs was the third baseman for the Reds during their winning 1939 and 1940 seasons and was another of those who frequented the Milders Inn and home. Born on April 22, 1910, in Caswell County, North Carolina, Riggs was on hand at the Milderses' in 1940, when teammates Harry Craft and Frank McCormick were married, even serving in the wedding party for McCormick. Likewise, the Milders family said it was Riggs who hit the baseball that landed in the lap of Ray Milders's daughter, Petie, and was the same baseball that Harry Craft had the whole team sign for her.

Reds third baseman Lew Riggs at Crosley Field. *Tully Milders family photo.*

Riggs did not start his professional career with the

Reds third baseman Lew Riggs in Ray Milders's backyard, 1939 or 1940. *Tully Milders family photo.*

Reds, instead getting his big break in 1934 with the St. Louis Cardinals. After being instrumental in helping the Cardinals win the 1934 World Series, Riggs was traded to Cincinnati in 1935 and remained there for the next six seasons, leading the team to the National League pennant win in 1939 and its World Series win in 1940. While with the Reds, Lew Riggs was also named to the All-Star team in 1936. In 1941, the Reds traded Riggs to the Brooklyn Dodgers, where he helped them win the National League championship. After leaving the team in 1942 to serve in World War II, Riggs never achieved the same level of skill when he returned to the Dodgers in 1946. He retired from the game in 1946, with a lifetime batting average of .262. Riggs, like his teammate Frank McCormick, eventually succumbed to cancer and died at age sixty-five in Durham, North Carolina, on August 12, 1975. The Milders family remembered Lew Riggs as a kind person with a great sense of humor who loved to join them at the picnics they held in their backyard. As for Riggs, he felt just as close to Ray and Margaret Milders as he did to the rest of his teammates, even signing a photo for them in 1940, calling Ray and Margaret "the best friends he ever had."

Though not as close to the Milderses as Craft, McCormick and Riggs, many other Reds players knew them well enough to call them friends, including the following superstars.

ERNIE LOMBARDI

According to the Baseball Hall of Fame website, Reds catcher Ernie Lombardi was the kind of player who made up team owners' dreams:

> *Everything about the long time Reds star seemed larger than life. He had one of the best arms in baseball, the kind of arm that tempted scouts at times to make him a pitcher. He had hands that seemed to almost make a catcher's mitt superfluous. He swung a 42 ounce bat that made everyone else's bats look like a toothpick, thanks to his massive wrists and forearms. Then there was his nose. A massive protuberance that earned him the almost inevitable nickname of "Schnozz," and there was his lack of speed. More than anything, Lombardi was one of the biggest and best hitters the game has ever seen.*

Lombardi, who was elected to the Hall of Fame in 1986, had a .300-plus batting average on ten different occasions and a lifetime average of .306 over his seventeen-year career. This was in spite of him being a very slow runner. He won batting titles in 1938 and 1942, making him the last catcher to do so until Joe Mauer did it in 2006. He was named the National League MVP in 1938 and was considered one of the main reasons the Reds won the National League pennant in 1939 and the World Series in 1940.

Born on April 6, 1908, in Oakland, California, Lombardi began his professional career with the Oakland Oaks at the age of eighteen, hitting .360 for many of the several years he spent there. He was called up to the Majors in 1931 with the Brooklyn Robins, and then in 1932, he was traded to the Reds, where he played for the next ten years. One of the highlights of the 1939 World Series, and a popular story told time and again at the bar at the Milders Inn, came when the Yankees' Charlie Keller slid home and, making contact with Lombardi, knocked him out. Lombardi, who later said it was "very hot" during the game, said he became dizzy during the incident, which he claimed was why he lost consciousness. Whatever the cause, Lombardi temporarily lost the nickname of "Schnozz" and instead became known as "Snooze" for his blackout behind home plate. Team member and Milders's friend Harry Craft once said of Lombardi: "He was the best right handed hitter I ever saw. He was an exceptional player in every way except running. If he hadn't been so slow he would have had an even better batting average."

Like Craft, McCormick, Riggs and many other Reds players, Ernie Lombardi spent much of his free time at the home of Ray and Margaret

Reds catcher Ernie Lombardi, 1939 or 1940. *Tully Milders family photo.*

Milders. As the Milderses' daughter, Petie, reminisced in 1995 with *Journal News* columnist Ercel Eaton, it was clear that she considered Lombardi among her closest friends: "We all became friends when they came out to my parents' inn—the Milders Inn, to eat. Many times they brought their sleeping bags so they could spend the night at our home and sleep on the patio [where it was cool]."

In 1942, Lombardi was traded to the Braves after having an off season with the Reds in 1941. The next year, he was traded to the New York Giants, where he spent his last five years in the Majors. Even in his last year in baseball at age thirty-nine, Ernie Lombardi was selected for the All-Star team and batted .282. Ernie Lombardi died on September 26, 1977, in Santa Cruz, California, after being named in the 1968 book *Heroes behind the Mask* as one of the ten greatest catchers of all time, proving once again that the top names in baseball defined the Milders Inn clientele, while being responsible for its continued success.

BILL MYERS, IVAL GOODMAN, JOE BEGGS AND GENE THOMPSON

In addition to Harry Craft, Frank McCormick, Lew Riggs and Ernie Lombardi, some of the Reds players who often stayed the night at the Milderses' home after dining and drinking at the inn were Bill Myers, Ival Goodman, Joe Beggs and Gene Thompson. Though there isn't as much information about their time with the family, Louise Stevenson Beeler wrote in the *Hamilton Journal* in 1962 that they were among the players who often spent summer evenings sleeping on the Milderses' patio to avoid the Cincinnati heat. In regard to their careers, each player made his own mark for the Reds, especially during the team's winning 1939 and 1940 seasons.

Bill Myers was an infielder and a pitcher for the Reds and spent his entire career with the club. Born on August 14, 1910, in Enola, Pennsylvania, William Harrison Myers, whom the Milderses called "Billy," became known by that nickname, which clearly indicated the close relationship he had with the family. With a lifetime batting average of .257, Myers's last game came on September 25, 1941. Interestingly, Myers's most notable achievement came in connection with his death, which occurred on April 10, 1995, when he was more than eighty-four years old. *The Baseball Almanac* lists him as one of the one hundred oldest living players of all time.

Ival Goodman was born on July 23, 1908, in Northview, Missouri. He broke into the big leagues on April 16, 1935, at the age of twenty-six and became an all-star right fielder for the club. Considered a key player for the Reds National League pennant win in 1939 and their World Series win in 1940, Goodman was eventually elected to the Cincinnati Reds Hall of Fame in 1959. After his career with the Reds, Goodman left the team when he was purchased by the Chicago Cubs. He finished out his career with the Cubs and had a lifetime batting average of .281. Goodman returned to Cincinnati after his retirement and lived the rest of his life here until his death on November 25, 1984, when he was buried in Cincinnati's Oakhill Cemetery. The Milderses, along with his fans, referred to Goodman by the nicknames "Goodie" and "Ol Mate" because of his pleasant disposition. Likewise, Ival Goodman was one of the players whom Hamilton author Bill Rentschler remembered meeting when he spent time at the Milders Inn as a boy.

Pitcher Joe Beggs, also known as "Fireman," was born on November 4, 1910, in Rankin, Pennsylvania. Although he wasn't considered a superstar, Beggs distinguished himself from other ballplayers throughout his ten-year career in several ways. First, he was noted for his intelligence and his ability to speak several languages and was one of the few baseball players at the time who had earned a college degree. He was likely the player who regaled the Milderses and their customers with stories about current events and other issues outside of baseball. Likewise, with his language proficiency, he got along quite well with the immigrants who still frequented the inn. Though Joe Beggs was known as a star athlete in college, his athletic accomplishments came in the sport of javelin rather than baseball, though he was fortunate to play on World Series teams in both the National and American Leagues. Though he didn't arrive in Cincinnati until 1940, his stint with the Reds became a significant turning point in his career, and he came here in time to join many of his fellow teammates on their various outings with the Milderses. Though he was used as a relief pitcher, Beggs made significant contributions to the Reds' World Series win in 1940, and though he only started in one game, he finished out the season with a record of 12-3 and an ERA of 2.00. After Joe Beggs retired from baseball, the later years of his life found him changing careers, and he spent several years teaching high school history and geography in the Cincinnati Public School system. In yet another strange connection between the Reds and the Milderses, Ray Milders also changed careers late in life, after the Milders Inn closed.

Gene Thompson was another Reds player who was listed by *Baseball Almanac* as one of the one hundred oldest living players of all time, living to the age of eighty-nine. Born in Latham, Illinois, on June 7, 1917, Eugene Earl Thompson was known as Junior by the Milderses and friends and fans alike. Thompson made his professional debut with the Reds farm team in 1935 and was a right-handed pitcher. Between 1939 and 1942, he had a record of thirty-nine wins and twenty-seven losses. Thompson was part of the 1940 World Series Reds team, though he had only one start and did not finish well in game five. After his career, Thompson became a scout for the San Francisco Giants and served in that capacity until he died forty years later on August 24, 2006.

Bucky Walters and Willard Hershberger

The most tragic story surrounding the Milderses and their relationship with the Cincinnati Reds involved Bucky Walters and Willard Hershberger. Though both players were part of the good times that many of the Reds had at the Milders family home, their story also surrounded the most tragic event in Reds history and remains one of the most devastating personal incidents that ever occurred for Ray and Margaret Milders.

Considered the premier pitcher in the National League and one of the best pitchers in the Majors between 1939 and 1946, William Henry "Bucky" Walters was born on April 19, 1909, in Philadelphia. Although Walters left high school in his sophomore year to become an electrician, he still played sandlot ball. After one of those games in the mid-1920s, scout Roy Ellum saw Walters play and asked him to come try out for the Piedmont League in Alabama. After borrowing ten dollars from his grandma to buy a suitcase, Walters went to Alabama and ended up playing for numerous minor-league teams before being signed by the Boston Braves, making his major-league debut in 1931. After playing for the Braves and then Montreal and then being sold to a San Francisco farm team, Walters had a short stint with the Phillies before being sold to the Reds in 1938.

Hershberger, meanwhile, was born on May 28, 1910, in Lemoncove, California, and debuted with the Reds in 1938. Serving as the backup catcher to superstar Ernie Lombardi, Hershberger was a short, small man, weighing only 167 pounds in comparison to Lombardi's 230. In spite of the difference in their size, Hershberger was inspired by Lombardi to develop his batting skills, and he ended up with a lifetime batting average of .316. Though he was considered by the team to be one of its best rookies, Willard Hershberger had long suffered from major depression as the result of his father killing himself twelve years before after a hunting trip the two had taken. Reportedly, his father used the gun that Hershberger had been using for sport. As a result of his depression, Willard Hershberger was emotionally unstable when he was forced to take over as the Reds' main catcher when Ernie Lombardi was injured in 1940.

Though Hershberger did a good job filling in for Lombardi and Bucky Walters was having the best season of his career, tragedy struck on July 31 when Walters, who was pitching against the New York Giants at the Polo Grounds, lost the game in the ninth inning after the Reds were up 4–1. Hershberger felt the loss was his fault, in spite of Walters's and Reds manager Bill McKechnie's insistence that he had nothing to do with it. Three days later, the Reds lost a double-header to Boston and Hershberger became even more distraught, once again blaming himself for both losses. He reportedly told third baseman Billy Werber that the Reds wouldn't have lost if Ernie Lombardi had been catching. After failing to field a bunt in the second game of the double-header, Hershberger alluded to his father's suicide, and after the game he told McKechnie that he was going to kill himself just like his father. McKechnie stayed with Hershberger until he calmed down and later told reporters that he believed at the time that Hershberger would be fine.

On August 3, however, Hershberger missed batting practice, telling McKechnie that he didn't feel well, which caused the manager to worry. As a result, McKechnie told Hershberger to come to practice in street clothes. When Hershberger didn't show up, McKechnie sent his fellow team member and friend Dan Cohen to the hotel to check on him. Upon arrival, Cohen found Hershberger's door locked, and after getting a hotel employee to open the room, Cohen found Hershberger dead in the bathtub with his jugular vein slit. Cohen said that Hershberger had spread towels around the bathroom floor before he died in an apparent attempt to create less of a mess as he bled to death. At just thirty years old, Hershberger remains the only player in baseball history to commit suicide while serving as an active player during the regular season.

After the news of his death broke, team manager Bill McKechnie called the players together and told them they needed to win the World Series for the man he called "Hershie." McKechnie never revealed all the details of his conversation with Hershberger as he tried to calm him down the day before he died, but he told reporters that "no one on the team was to blame for his death." Willard Hershberger's stunned teammates returned home to Cincinnati after the announcement and ended up winning the World Series against Detroit. The team gave part of its World Series earnings to Hershberger's mother, a sum that reportedly totaled $5,803.

Like the Reds players, Hershberger's friends the Milderses were devastated by the news of his death, with a cloud of darkness and depression hanging over the inn for months. According to Ray Milders's grandson Tully, his family was on hand a few days later for the Crosley Field memorial service for Hershberger, and he said they also hosted a small wake at the inn to pay tribute to his memory:

> *My grandparents were invited to the memorial service for Willard Hershberger and they joined the fans and players who stood at attention for a moment of silence before the Reds and Cubs game, not long after he committed suicide. They said that a huge bouquet of flowers was placed at home plate in honor of Hershberger, and even the umpires removed their hats and stood at attention during the memorial. Later, my grandparents hosted a small wake at the Milders Inn for those players who often joined Hershberger at their home for picnics and parties and who were devastated by his loss.*

Though the Milders family and the Reds players moved on after Hershberger's death, lingering questions and the subsequent sadness over their loss affected them for years to come. In his 1991 article in *Sports Illustrated*, William Nack also recounted the impact that Hershberger's suicide had on the team, and he said it even played a big part in Ernie Lombardi's eventual suicide attempt after his own playing days were over. In spite of this tragic incident, the Milders family remembers the happy stories about Hershberger and the Reds who called the Milders Inn their second home. Though most of the players were just starting out when they befriended the Milderses, they were also the very superstars who were responsible for the amazing 1939 and '40 seasons, which according to many continue to be the two most underrated Reds teams in the history of the franchise. Though the years of the Reds and Milders parties and picnics were few, the stories of their eating at the inn and then sleeping at Ray and Margaret Milders's home are among the very stories that still have folks around this area talking about the Milders Inn today.

Chapter 6

RAY

The Later Years

While 1940 and '41 saw the Reds players continuing to spend their free time at the Milders Inn, World War II brought an end to an era for the ballplayers, as well as for the Milderses. The thrill of the 1940 Reds' World Series win and subsequent marriages of Frank McCormick and Harry Craft at Ray Milders's home were fading, and once again, joy gave way to sorrow when Mom Milders died on December 7, 1942. As Mom was buried in Hamilton's Rose Hill Cemetery alongside her husband, Jake, there was a feeling of great loss for those who knew the Milderses in the beginning. Likewise, by then, World War II was underway, and most of the Milderses' ballplayer friends had either left the Reds for other teams or were in the final stage of their own careers. May 1942 also brought food rationing to America when the U.S. Office of Price Administration froze prices on everyday goods starting with sugar and coffee. Mandatory rationing was next put into place for these and many more items, and each American family received ration books and tokens that dictated how much gasoline, tires, sugar, meat, silk, shoes, nylon, coffee, cheese, stoves and processed foods they could buy. Ultimately, food rationing meant that Ray Milders could not buy the volume of food he needed to keep the Milders Inn running successfully. With Mom and Jake Milders now gone and the food shortages causing financial problems, Ray Milders decided to close the inn in October 1942. Sadly, the restaurant that held the memories of the Prohibition gangsters, the superstars of the Cincinnati Reds and the mellow singing voices of Ray Milders and Dud Mecum became just another memory of days gone by. In

An abandoned Milders Inn in 1955 just before the City of Fairfield tore it down. *Tully Milders family photo.*

November of that year, the furnishings were put up for auction, and patrons rushed in to buy the thirty tables and kitchen equipment that symbolized much of their young adulthood. Perhaps the auctioneer's bill of sale said it best when, in bold headlines, it read: "**Ohio's Best Known Steak and Chicken Restaurant**." Sadly, for the next thirteen years, the restaurant that brought so much joy and fame to the region sat empty as the community in which it stood went through dramatic changes of its own, and Fairfield Township became the city of Fairfield in 1955.

With the changes brought about by World War II and the growth of the region, remaining Fairfield Township was no longer an option for the local civic leaders of the community. In 1953, the city of Hamilton started to recognize the value of the township land, and the chamber of commerce published a map with the intent to push for the annexation of the township into the city. The map indicated that the Hamilton border would extend south beyond Nilles Road and west beyond Gilmore. The chamber launched a campaign to convince the residents of Fairfield Township that becoming part of Hamilton would mean lower utility rates, better street maintenance and increased property values. However, Fairfield Township residents didn't agree, and they saw an annexation with Hamilton as indicative of the loss of industrial revenue, the loss of their school system and the lost opportunity for self-government. On July 10, 1954, concerned township residents formed a village to keep the city of Hamilton at bay, and by way of a special census, they formed the city of Fairfield on October 20, 1955.

One of the first things the new city government decided to do was tear down abandoned buildings for a beautification project, and as a result, the long since abandoned Milders Inn was finally demolished. Likewise, the 1960s brought about a decade of rapid growth for Fairfield, and the fields near the site of the former Milders Inn were paved and made into busy streets as the population exploded. The same area where Turkey Joe Jacobs died after a dramatic ambush twenty-six years before now housed a new post office and high school with expanded protection from the police and fire departments. Likewise, the Milderses' ground that grew much of the produce for the inn became the site for restaurants and small businesses that still remain today. With the inn gone and the surrounding area now permanently changed, Ray Milders's daughter-in-law, Marlene Milders Sloneker, said that there was an initial negative impact on Ray's psyche that was brought about by the inn's closure. But she said that like his father, Jake, who was forced to start over after the 1913 flood, Ray also started over and had several other successful business ventures later in life. Sloneker said that in spite of his success in these various other careers, music always remained Ray's first love, and he remained committed to singing until the day he died: "Ray always enjoyed his position as the patriarch of the family. He was handsome and was close to my children. Ray more than anything wanted to be a singer, and after the inn closed, in more recent years, he would bring Dud Mecum to our house and they would continue to entertain us."

Following his years at the Milders Inn, Ray next became the owner of Sunbrite Laundry and Dry Cleaning in Hamilton in the late 1940s. Milders rented the building where the laundry was located on Hanover Street. During these years, many Hamilton homes didn't have washers and dryers, in spite of the fact that the patent for the first electric washer had been awarded to Alva Fisher back in 1910. Even Maytag's invention of an electric washing machine with an agitator in 1922 didn't create a local rise in purchases for homeowners. With Ray Milders's inheritance of his father's and grandfather's business acumen, he decided to meet this unfulfilled need of local housewives and did quite well until 1960. By then, Hamilton had finally caught up with the rest of the country, and most families had electric washers and dryers in their homes. As business began to decline, Ray decided it was time to move on, so he closed Sunbrite Laundry and Dry Cleaning for good.

After closing the dry cleaners, Ray Milders found success at yet another career at the age of sixty. Knowing local realtor Mel Sirk, Ray began to successfully sell real estate, even winning numerous awards for being a top agent in Hamilton and Butler County. Tully Milders said he still comes across people today who bought their homes from his grandfather: "From my memory, Ray loved selling homes and over the years when introducing myself to people and explaining my connection to Ray, they told me they were in their homes because of his trustworthiness as a realtor."

Tully Milders, like his mother, Marlene, said Ray never completely got over his days at the Milders Inn. He remembered as a boy going to Shady Nook, another popular local restaurant known for its large Wurlitzer organ, where his grandfather would often get up and sing:

> *We would get glimpses of his love for the Milders Inn when we went to dinner with him. Often, at Shady Nook, Ray would get up and begin singing to the folks who were dining that night with Stan Todd playing organ. Then after several songs we would have folks visit our table and talk to Ray about the old days at the Milders Inn. In fact, anytime old friends or relatives would visit my grandparents, the stories would start, and if a former musician acquaintance was in town they would come to my parents' house with Ray and play and sing just like in the old days. Even today there are still a few folks around who ate at the inn, and I still occasionally run into someone who will share a story with me about the inn. The most recent example came when a man came into Ryan's* [the tavern he manages] *and told me that as a small child he would sneak up to the fence at the inn and look through it into the garden. He wanted to watch everything that was going on so he could hear the music and catch a glimpse of his favorite Reds ballplayers.*

Tully, who called Ray Milders "Gabbo," said his fondest childhood memories came when Ray would bring local celebrity singer Dud Mecum to his house, spending hours regaling the family with his favorite tunes. Ray ended up becoming somewhat of a father figure to his grandson when, in a strange turn of events, he outlived his son (and Tully's father) Bill, just as his own father, Jake, had outlived his sister Helen decades before. William "Bill" Milders, like his great-aunt, died at age thirty-nine after suffering from an aneurysm. His death came eight years before that of his father, Ray, continuing a Milders family tragedy in which the fathers lived to see the death of at least one child.

On February 2, 1980, Ray Milders suffered a heart attack and died at age seventy-nine. Folks from across the region came to pay their final respects to the man who made such an important mark on Hamilton and Butler County's history. Sadly, Tully Milders was living in California when his grandfather died, pursuing his own dream of restaurant ownership. Though Tully never got over missing his grandfather's funeral, it was ultimately Ray's death that brought him back to this area to begin a path that would eventually bring the Milders Inn back to life.

Part III
Today

Chapter 7
TULLY

The Early Years of a Budding Restaurateur

On August 15, 1957, Ray Milders's son William and his wife, Marlene, welcomed their son William Jr. into the world. Known by his friends and family as "Tully," he continues to keep the Milders Inn food and stories alive at Hamilton's Ryan's Tavern, where he now works as the general manager. Each Monday night, Tully and his mother, Marlene, work hard to share the food and stories from the Milders Inn with Ryan's customers. What makes the evenings special is that the recipes are the same, the kitchen utensils are the same and the rave reviews are the same when each dinner is finished. Tully remembers:

> *I was fascinated by the Milders Inn and how it kept me connected to my family and their story. My aunt Petie kept all of the stories alive from when Ray ran the inn, talking about her memories of hanging out on a balcony above the entrance to see folks come in and out and how she fell in love with my uncle when he entered in his Marine uniform. My grandfather Ray was close to me as a kid, and with his working at the inn and Petie keeping the stories alive, I decided to make restaurant work my career and life.*

In addition to the Milders Inn stories being the reason Tully Milders went into the restaurant business, he also felt his dad's death at age thirty-nine was brought on by an inactive lifestyle. Tully said that his father's job as an

Tully Milders and his mother, Marlene Milders Sloneker, awaiting the crowds with a plate of Mom Milders's fried chicken on Milders Inn night at Ryan's Tavern, 2015. *Captured Beauty Photography.*

accountant required him to sit behind a desk, and as a teen, he vowed never to follow that path, instead learning to develop a farm-to-table meal plan that would help others live a healthier life: "I was a kid, and I blamed my dad's death on his sitting behind a desk and getting heavy. I vowed I wouldn't sit behind a desk in my career, and with my grandfather Ray's restaurant experience at the inn, I took a job at McDonald's in Hamilton, becoming the assistant manager by age sixteen."

Tully remained at the local McDonald's for five years, winning regional awards for customer service. He credits his grandfather Ray for instilling in him a strong love of people, and he wanted to offer a dining experience to customers that they wouldn't forget. After leaving McDonald's, Tully moved to another popular local restaurant, the Hickory Hut, known throughout the area for home-style favorites such as meatloaf, mashed potatoes and homemade fruits and cobblers—the same type of food that was popular at the Milders Inn. Tully first served as a line cook and then as a meat cutter, chicken fryer and baker. He remembered his favorite day on that job came when his grandfather Ray visited to taste his food and compared his grandson's career to his own:

> *Ray came in for dinner at the Hickory Hut a year before he died. He ate my food, and I was very proud. He asked if he could come to the back to visit the kitchen, and as I came out to get him, I slipped and flipped a pan of meat sauce that had been heated to 350 degrees. My skin blistered as the hot sauce poured over me, but I still had to make the meals for the guests. I remember Ray's eyes got big, and as I ripped my shirt off, uncovering more of my blistered skin, he simply said that "my food was good."*

In 1979, twenty-two-year-old Tully Milders channeled the discontent of his great-great-grandfather Peter when, in spite of his success, he began feeling restless at his job at the Hickory Hut. As a result, he decided to take a vacation to Los Angeles with his best friend. After enjoying the trip and not wanting to return to the Hickory Hut job, he decided to stay for good, as he loved the California lifestyle. Once again relying on his family's background in the restaurant business, Tully became the co-owner of the then popular restaurant in Manhattan Beach called the Back-Bay Restaurant. Once again, drama occurred, but this time it wasn't scalding meat sauce; it was a customer. Tully towed a lady's car from the side of his restaurant where she was illegally parked. Enraged by the fine from the tow, the woman sued Tully, and they ended up hashing it out on the popular TV show *The People's Court.* Tully won his case. With his family tendency to befriend celebrities, Tully next ended up hiring Ron Fields as a server at the Back-Bay, and it turned out that the young man was the grandson of famed actor W.C. Fields. Tully said that Ron Fields had many of the same destructive habits that made his grandfather famous.

Throughout Tully, Ray, Jake and even Peter Milders's lives, joy had a way of turning to tragedy for the family, and in 1980, that old pattern returned. That was the year Ray Milders died and Tully lost his beloved father figure and grandpa. His mother, Marlene, a widow for several years after Bill Milders's untimely death, also decided to remarry. Deciding that he had missed too much of the Milders family life while living in California, Tully came back to Hamilton and, by 1982, was working as a meat cutter and lunch cook at the newly opened Red River Cattle Company. The restaurant, another local favorite, became famous for offering a six-pound steak dinner challenge in which the meal was free (instead of $26.99) to anyone who could eat it in one hour and fifteen minutes. After six months, his former bosses came calling from the Hickory Hut, this time offering him the job of general manager. After putting his original discontent aside and returning to the restaurant, Tully met the owner's daughter Marcy, who managed the front of the house. The two began dating and ultimately were married. Many of their staff became their second family, just as Jake and Mom's and Ray and Margaret's staff were their families. Tully recalls: "We were a tight group at the Hickory Hut, and several of the staff now work for me here at Ryan's, helping with Milders Inn night. I served there as general manager between 1982 and 1988 and tried to show the same compassion that my great-grandparents had by hiring many single mothers and other folks who were down on their luck."

THE CASE HOUSE

In 1988, the Hickory Hut sold, and the new owners changed the menu and entire concept of the restaurant. Tully remained as general manager during the transition, but once again, he was restless and unhappy with the change, and his sadness turned to sorrow on March 1, 1989, when his grandmother Margaret died at Fort Hamilton Hospital, bringing an end to the third generation of the Milders family. It was at this point that Tully Milders decided to leave the Hickory Hut for good. He then joined the staff as the operations manager of another one of Hamilton's historic restaurants, Richard's Pizza. Richard's, founded in 1955 by Hamiltonian Richard Underwood, became famous for its Italian Steak Sandwich, which is still shipped around the world. After Tully's short stint there, the early to mid-1990s saw him working at a variety of Butler County restaurants, including Attractions, a restaurant/bar near the campus of Miami University, his grandfather Ray's alma mater (now known as 45 East Bar & Grill); and the student-supported bars the Saloon and First Run. Though he spent about six years in bar management, Tully never lost the desire to own his own restaurant, and his love for the Milders Inn instilled in him a continuing love of restaurant history that he wanted to preserve. In 1996, Tully, and a co-worker from Attractions bought a Victorian-style home at the corner of Main and Eighth Streets in downtown Brookville, Indiana, where his mother Marlene's family was from. Built in 1875, the structure was the site of the former office of a dentist named Case. (As an aside, Dr. Case was reportedly a cousin of Orville and Wilber Wright, and his mother spent fourteen years living in captivity with the Shawnee Indians.) With the history that was tied to the building and to the Case family, Tully decided that it would be the perfect location to house a historical restaurant that served period foods. As a result, he spent quite a bit of time researching recipes from the 1870s, and they were the only meals he served at the Case House. During his years as owner of the restaurant, Tully was recognized by several national magazines and the restaurant was listed as one of the top seven in Greater Cincinnati. Polly Campbell, the well-known food critic at the *Cincinnati Enquirer*, said a trip to the Case House was like taking a trip back in time:

> *Sunday dinner at the Case House in Brookville, Indiana made me think of the novel "Time and Again," by Jack Finney. The hero of this time travel mystery surrounded himself so completely with authentic items from life in 19th century New York that he was transported back to that era. After sitting for a time in the parlor of the 1875 building, eating the kind of foods available in a small Indiana town of that day, I envision all the satellite dishes* [now] *in town disappearing and the sound of* cars whizzing by on the street outside changing to the clip clop of horses. [Though there was] *no such luck, I did feel transported in one important way—I'd gone back to a time when people knew how to cook without a freezer, a microwave, or a can opener.*

Tully Milders said that it was during the time that he owned the Case House that he once again began to channel his great-grandparents' love of the farm-to-table concept:

> *At the Case House, I grew my own herbs, which we used in the historical recipes, and it was there that I decided to follow in Jake and Mom Milders's footsteps by relying on local farmers to supply my produce. What I didn't grow, I bought locally, and this is a practice that I still use here at Ryan's today. The Case House is where I also began making Mom Milders's fried chicken to serve to the diners of today.*

Though Tully admitted that his interpretation of a nineteenth-century menu wasn't a strict one, he did not serve Jell-O, French fries, canned soup, portabella mushrooms or anything that became popular in the recent past. As such, one clearly sees his connection to Mom Milders when she refused to serve hamburgers, yellow corn or margarine to guests in the early years at the Milders Inn. The iron skillets he used to make the Case House special corn muffins and the Milders Inn fried chicken were the same ones used by Mom at the Milders Inn, a gift from Tully's aunt Petie that transcended the generations. Other specialty historical dishes served at the Case House that inspired Tully to create the current Milders Inn–inspired menu at Ryan's included Yankee pot roast, roasted half chicken with almond sauce, corn fritters with added kernels of corn to give them a crunchy coating that tasted like hush puppies, maple-glazed pork chops, baked trout, stewed apples, sage dressing and, for dessert, homemade peach cobbler, raspberry pecan bars and devil's food cake. Though the Case House proved successful for Tully and his partners, Brookville is built around a large man-made lake that attracts tourists throughout the summer months. However, in the winter, the area is nearly desolate, and as a result, it was hard for Tully to keep the doors open. Like the impact that World War II had on his grandfather Ray, the unfortunate lack of year-round tourism brought about hard financial times, and Tully closed the restaurant in 2000.

RYAN'S TAVERN AND THE REBIRTH OF THE MILDERS INN

In 2003, Tully Milders was divorced and remarried to his current wife, Hamiltonian Teri Glynn, and she talked him into moving to Florida. With his restaurant now closed, Tully agreed, and he took a job with the popular chain restaurant Cracker Barrel. After management training at Cracker Barrel's headquarters in Lebanon, Tennessee, Tully was sent to Daytona Beach, Florida, where he managed the store across from the Daytona International Speedway. Thinking that the large crowds of race fans would be too much for him to handle, Tully asked for a transfer and moved to St. Augustine, Florida. What he didn't know was that the St. Augustine location was actually the busiest Cracker Barrel in Florida, and he was forced to work well over sixty hours per week. Soon after, he met the area director of Bennigan's International Irish Pub, and this became the catalyst for his return back to Hamilton. Bennigan's offered Tully a job as one of the managers in Jacksonville, meaning more money and fewer hours. He accepted, and that is where he spent the next five years of his career until 2006. Bennigan's is also where he got experience working in an Irish pub atmosphere, which later helped him land his current job at Ryan's Tavern. With both Tully's and his wife's roots being here, they decided to return home in 2006, as both missed their families who still lived in town. It was because of this move that, in a few short years, the Milders Inn was reborn.

In 2007, then Hamilton mayor Don Ryan was working with the city council to create a downtown arts and entertainment district as an attempt to revitalize the local economy. Around the same time, Ryan, a seventh-generation Irishman, watched a PBS special about the popularity of Irish pubs across the globe, remembering that "pub" in Irish was short for "public house," meaning a place that serves alcohol but where the discussion often turns to God, politics and family. Ryan, himself a lover of these ideals, as well as history, liked the possibility of putting a historical restaurant in a historical building. Since he was working as mayor to revitalize Hamilton,

The exterior of Ryan's Tavern at 241 High Street in Hamilton, Ohio. The building was constructed in 1890. *Captured Beauty Photography.*

Ryan's Tavern on Milders Inn night, 2015. *Captured Beauty Photography.*

which had become very run-down due to the decline of the American era of industrialization, it made sense that he create a nice restaurant that local citizens would enjoy. As a result, he bought the historical structure at 241 High Street, which was built in 1890. It first housed a general store, then an F.W. Woolworth from the 1920s to the 1950s, Martin's Dress Shop from the 1950s to the 1980s and Dunlap's Men's Clothing from the 1980s until 2006. Ryan felt his newly acquired building was the perfect place for Hamiltonians to enjoy an Irish tavern of their own:

> *When I saw the PBS special, I thought, "Why can't we do that here?" So after getting the building at a great price, I first decided to rent it while I worked out the financials, and then after a year, my accountant reminded me that I originally thought Hamilton needed an Irish tavern. So after getting my wife's agreement, I decided to build the tavern that we have today. At first, I was only going to use the first floor, but since I have a four-story building, I now use the bottom two floors for the public and the top two for storage. Likewise, I needed a kitchen, so I bought the building next door, which was a former restaurant, and I then converted them both into one building.*

Former Hamilton mayor and tavern owner Don Ryan in the new home of the Milders Inn, 2015. *Captured Beauty Photography.*

Ryan said that he and his wife visited Ireland many times when deciding to open the tavern, as they wanted it to be historically accurate. He said it took two years to renovate the building, and he redid the brick outside to make the exterior look like it did in the 1890s. Ryan's wife, Vickie, herself an author, wrote the menus, filling them with family history, and Tully Milders was hired, becoming instrumental in planning the Irish/American menu. Tully said Don Ryan hired him because of his extensive restaurant background and his experience at Bennigan's: "I couldn't be prouder to work here at Ryan's," said Milders. "With my own family history and experience at Bennigan's, I'm once again able to provide the best quality service and the best quality food here at Ryan's, just like my great-grandparents and grandparents did at the Milders Inn."

As time went on, Ryan's became successful, and Hamilton began to bounce back. The restaurant still continues to be known as the "nicest in town." However, though he was successful in his new position as a tavern manager, Tully Milders never lost the desire to share his family history with the community, and he desperately wanted to share the delicious food that made his grandparents famous. As a result, in 2013, when Tully and Don Ryan identified the fact that Monday night was the slowest night at Ryan's,

The banquet room in Ryan's Tavern. *Captured Beauty Photography.*

they decided to search for a special menu to bring in the crowds. At first, Hamilton resident Gina Isgro—herself a significant part of Hamilton's restaurant history, and a descendent of a local Italian family who owned a popular Hamilton restaurant many years before—created Isgro's night at Ryan's. In the 1970s, it was Isgro's that was the nicest restaurant in town, and when Gina brought the recipes back for Isgro's night at Ryan's, the crowds came in to reminisce and enjoy the delicious food that made hers a local household name. In fact, Gina's night became so popular at the tavern that she developed her own clientele and as a result, decided to open her own new restaurant nearby. While Don Ryan and Tully Milders were happy for Gina's success, they were once again without a special menu for the slowest night of the week. However, now that Gina was gone, Tully quickly realized that Hamiltonians liked the idea of promoting the city's restaurant history, and he decided that the time had finally come for him to bring back the Milders Inn:

> *When Gina left, I knew that we needed something similar at Ryan's to fill our seats on Monday nights. Throughout my time here at Ryan's, I'd had people asking me to start serving home-cooked food like we had back in my Hickory Hut days, and since I had all of Mom Milders's cast-iron skillets*

> *and other cooking utensils, and since home-style cooking like they had at the Milders Inn is in my comfort zone, we started serving the Milders Inn chicken. I'd always wanted to share Mom's food and the Milders memories, and as a result, Milders Inn night at Ryan's was born.*

In addition to a need for history and great food, the timing of Gina Isgro's leaving was perfect in another way. The year 2013 marked the 100th anniversary of the 1913 flood that devastated Jake Milders family, leading him to open the Milders Inn in the first place. As a result, with Milders Inn night at Ryan's in place, Tully Milders's history came full circle, and the current generation gets to enjoy the stories and the food that made that history famous. Since its inception, Tully has worked to bring much of the Milders memorabilia into Ryan's, and one corner of the tavern is now a small exhibit space devoted to Jake, Mom, Ray and those who made the Milders Inn a significant part of local restaurant history. Though he has no relation to Tully or the Milders family, Don Ryan said it thrills him when people come into his tavern and tell him they feel like they're home, a concept that originally brought success to the Milderses and likewise continues to bring success to the Ryans: "It's so cool when someone walks in, whether it's Milders night or any other, and you hear a shriek because they have seen someone they haven't seen in years. It happens all the time, and it's why I opened the tavern in the first place."

Because of the family-like atmosphere, Ryan's is now the hot spot for those looking to host wedding rehearsals, class reunions and other special events. Another similarity between Ryan's and the Milders Inn comes in the famous visitors who regularly stop by. Hamilton, Ohio, has become a popular spot for production companies, with several films having been produced around downtown. As such, just like when the gangsters, musicians and Cincinnati Reds stopped into the Milders Inn so many years ago, one can now see the occasional celebrity in the booths of Ryan's Tavern. Tully comments:

> *In May of this year, the actor James Franco [127 Hours,* 2010*; Freaks & Geeks,* 1999] *produced part of the upcoming movie* The Long Home *here in Hamilton, and he, along with actresses Courtney Love [The People vs. Larry Flynt,* 1996] *and Zoe Levin [The Way Way Back,* 2013] *and actors Josh Hutcherson [The Hunger Games: Mockingjay Part 1,* 2013], *Ashton Kutcher [The Butterfly Effect,* 2004; *That 70's Show,* 1998] *and Garret Dillahunt [No Country for Old Men,* 2007], *regularly came into the tavern, and I'm sure they enjoyed Mom Milders's chicken.*

> *Likewise, another exciting moment for me as a member of the Milders family occurred not too long ago, when former Reds centerfielder Herm Winningham stopped by on Milders Inn night to try the foods that the Reds from the 1940s enjoyed. He loved looking at the pictures of his past teammates, and he loved the food that made the Milders Inn great.*

Winningham played for the Montreal Expos, the Boston Red Sox, the New York Mets and the Cincinnati Reds, making his debut in September 1984 and finishing his career in late 1992. During his tenure in Cincinnati, he played for the 1990 National League Champions Reds team before being traded to the Red Sox to finish out his career. With a lifetime batting average of .239, Winningham returned to his hometown of Orangeburg, South Carolina, after his career, and he currently serves as the head baseball coach of the local high school team. When he had the opportunity to visit Hamilton, he told Tully Milders he made a special trip to Ryan's to taste the Milders Inn chicken because he had heard so much about it when playing for the Reds. Tully said it made him proud to know that the connection between his family and Cincinnati baseball continues.

In addition to a successful restaurant career that rivals that of his family, Tully Milders, now fifty-eight, has several children of his own. His son Phil is following in his footsteps as a budding restaurateur. Just like his dad, Phil works for Cracker Barrel, and Tully hopes that he will keep the Milders Inn stories alive for future generations. He said that in addition to the pride that comes from sharing his family history, he wants people to know that Hamilton and Fairfield, Ohio, have long, important histories that reach out to the four corners of the globe.

As Tully continues growing Milders Inn night at Ryan's, the Hamilton and Fairfield areas remain full of people who visited the restaurant when Tully's grandfather Ray hosted the Reds and made beautiful music there. Though the patrons who knew Mom and Jake have long since passed, the fried chicken that started it all back in 1914 remains as popular today as it did at the beginning. With 165 years' worth of history in the books, including fascinating tales of food, music, gangsters and baseball, the Milders Inn is more than the story of a local restaurant from days gone by. It is the story of struggle and success, drama and good times, joy and sorrow, and as such, it is the ultimate story of how one family had the courage to pick up after life handed them several major blows, and how that courage changed the history and the landscape of the communities they called home.

Part IV
Recipes and Cooking Tips

Chapter 8

FROM THE MILDERS INN

Though the fried chicken was the star at the Milders Inn, Mom Milders's cooking style and many of her side dishes survived the generations and are used by her great-grandson Tully today. The whole process of re-creating a Milders Inn–style experience through the serving of historical recipes started for Tully Milders at his Case House restaurant. That process continues on Milders Inn night, when he also serves historical Irish recipes created especially for Monday nights at Ryan's Tavern. The following recipes are a compilation of the customer favorites from all three historical restaurants. Though the measurements are designed for larger crowds, Tully Milders said they can be altered for home use by using one-fourth of the quantities listed. The areas where they can be altered are noted.

Mom Milders's Homemade Pickle Recipe

pickling cucumbers, sliced for jar storage
1 gallon white vinegar (Heinz)
1 quart water
¾ cup salt
3 tablespoons spice mix
1 teaspoon alum (McCormick)

½ teaspoon full saccharine (or saccharine tablets, which can be purchased at drugstores and crushed)
1 canister Coleman's dry mustard

Place pickling cucumbers in jars. Mix remaining ingredients and bring mixture to a boil. Pour the mixture over the cold cucumbers and seal. Store pickles for a minimum of eight weeks before eating. Refrigerate after opening.

MOM MILDERS'S MILK GRAVY

(recipe for 10 or more; use one-fourth of quantities listed for daily home use)
1½ pounds butter, melted
3 cups flour
1½ gallons whole milk
fried chicken cracklings
2 tablespoons salt
3 tablespoons white pepper

Make a roux (Milders Inn style): melt the butter in a saucepan over medium heat. As the butter reaches temperature, add the flour. As the flour bubbles, let it begin to make a paste to remove the flour taste, but don't let it brown. Set roux aside.

Heat the milk and, as it begins to boil, thicken it with the roux as your fried chicken comes out of the skillet. Remove from heat as soon as it thickens. Scrape the cracklings out of the skillet into the milk mixture and add the salt and white pepper. The breading on the chicken cracklings will also add seasoning to the milk gravy. Tully Milders said that while his great-grandmother Mom Milders never would have used instant potatoes, the milk gravy is suitable for use with the potatoes of your choice.

Marlene Milders Sloneker tasting Mom Milders's milk gravy at Milders Inn night at Ryan's Tavern, 2015. *Captured Beauty Photography.*

Milders Inn Cooking Tips

1. Crispy Milders Inn–Style Chicken

Tully Milders's mother, Marlene, takes special care to mix the spices before double battering the chicken breasts and placing them on the frying sheets that then go to Tully. While the exact spices that are used in the recipe will remain a secret kept by the remaining Milders family members, Tully did offer a few suggestions for those wanting something similar at home. He suggests the following:

First, fry chicken over medium heat until golden brown. For the first 10 minutes, heat it slowly on medium heat. As the chicken begins to color, turn it at approximately 23 minutes, and keep it on medium heat for a second 13 minutes more until the second side is cooked through. For the last 10 minutes, turn the heat back to medium-high heat, finishing the process when the chicken is golden brown and crispy. Total time: 46 minutes. For a crispy batter, Milders suggests dredging the chicken in whole milk, buttermilk and flour and then through a breading of your choice of spices. He suggests double breading the chicken to make it extra crispy, like the recipe used by

Marlene Milders Sloneker preparing the batter for Mom Milders's fried chicken at Milders Inn night at Ryan's Tavern, 2015. She is pictured in stage 1 of preparation. *Captured Beauty Photography.*

Marlene Milders Sloneker adding the second layer of batter (stage 2). *Captured Beauty Photography.*

Left: From the second coat of batter to the pan (stage 3). *Captured Beauty Photography.*

Below: Marlene Milders Sloneker dredging the chicken (stage 4). *Captured Beauty Photography.*

Tully Milders frying Mom Milders's fried chicken (stage 1 of the cooking process). *Captured Beauty Photography.*

Tully Milders frying chicken the same way Mom Milders did, using several cast-iron skillets at once (stage 2). *Captured Beauty Photography.*

Mom Milders's fried chicken in the pan (stage 3). *Captured Beauty Photography.*

Mom Milders. Milders also said that it is very important to have the oil heated in a cast-iron frying pan before dredging the chicken, as it needs to go right onto the fire versus sitting on a plate for a while before heating.

2. Freezing—Milders Inn–Style Green Beans

(For use with the Case House Green Bean Recipe on page 128)

Though Mom Milders and her staff canned green beans versus freezing them, Tully Milders and his Ryan's Tavern staff freeze them today. To successfully freeze green beans, he suggests the following:

Use a stringless bean such as Blue Lake Stringless, which are available at most farmers' markets in this region. After cleaning the beans, boil them in water for 3 minutes, then strain them until they are completely cool. After cooling, place them in small freezer bags until full and freeze until ready to serve.

3. Freezing—Milders Inn–Style White Corn

Though Mom Milders thought yellow corn was "horse corn," she canned hundreds of cans of Silver Queen corn each year. Today, due to health laws affecting American restaurants, Tully Milders freezes Milders-style corn for

Mom Milders's fried chicken, homemade cucumber salad and homemade mashed potatoes with milk gravy at Milders Inn night at Ryan's Tavern, 2015. *Captured Beauty Photography.*

his guests to enjoy at Milders Inn night at Ryan's. He suggests the following for home freezing:

Parboil 18 ears of white Silver Queen corn per batch. After 3 minutes of parboiling, cut the corn off the cob and let cool completely. After cooling, put in freezer bags but do not put anything besides the corn in each bag. Freeze until ready to serve. Tully suggests freezing enough corn to serve a family of four two times a month throughout the winter.

Chapter 9

RYAN'S TAVERN

Historical Irish Dishes

These dishes are served alongside the Milders Inn fried chicken today.

Ryan's Shepherd Pie

(recipe for 10 or more; use one-fourth of quantities listed for daily home use)

10 pounds ground beef
2 gallons water
¼ cup Kitchen Bouquet Browning Sauce
¼ cup Worcestershire sauce
2 cups chopped onion
2 cups chopped celery
½ cup beef paste
2 tablespoons onion salt
2 tablespoons ground black pepper
1 teaspoon garlic salt
1 pack frozen peas and carrots
1 small box cornstarch
Milders Inn–style mashed potatoes
parmesan cheese and parsley to taste

Sauté beef until cooked through and drain. Add water and next nine ingredients and bring to a boil. Thicken with cornstarch. After mixture is thickened, place a generous helping in an oven-safe bowl and then take a helping of the Milders Inn–style mashed potatoes and put on top. Top with parmesan cheese and parsley and put in oven for 3 minutes to brown and melt the cheese. Serve hot.

RYAN'S FISH AND CHIPS

(this recipe serves 4 as is)

1 Icelandic cod filet weighing 2½ to 3 pounds
4 cups whole milk
4 eggs
1 box Drake's breading mix (or coarse cornmeal if breading mix unavailable)

Cut the fish into 3 long, 10-ounce strips. Dredge the fish into an egg wash made from the milk and eggs. Roll the dredged fish in the breading mix or cornmeal and drop in a deep fryer for 4½ minutes. Serve with French fries or potato of choice.

RYAN'S REUBEN SANDWICH

(recipe is for 1 sandwich)

2 cups mayonnaise
½ cup catsup
¼ cup dill pickle relish
1 tablespoon dry mustard
4½ ounces shaved Certified Angus corned beef
2 slices thick swirled rye bread
2 slices Swiss cheese
2 ounces fresh sauerkraut

For the dressing, mix the mayonnaise, catsup, pickle relish and dry mustard and set aside.

Place the corned beef on the bread and melt the Swiss cheese, placing on top of the corned beef. Add the sauerkraut and drizzle with the homemade dressing to taste.

Chapter 10

THE CASE HOUSE

Historical Recipes from the Late Nineteenth Century

Though Tully Milders did his own research on these particular recipes as opposed to obtaining them directly from the Milders Inn, their connection to the Milderses is that they were popular during the early lives of Mom and Jake. The desserts in particular represent the types of pies and cakes made from the fresh fruit grown by local farmers who were known to the Milderses. Likewise, the practice of growing his own herbs and some vegetables in the Case House garden for these recipes came to Tully from the early members of the Milders family.

Sauces, Gravy and Meat

The Case House Yankee Pot Roast

1 4-pound boneless chuck roast, trimmed
1 tablespoon salt
1 tablespoon pepper
¼ cup flour
1½ pounds red potatoes
½ pound carrots
½ pound celery
½ pound red onions

Heat oil in a large skillet on medium heat. Sear roast, adding salt, pepper and flour to the meat and making sure that the oil covers only the bottom portion of the skillet. After the roast has browned, add potatoes and carrots. Reduce heat to a low simmer after 20 minutes and add remaining vegetables. Simmer on low for another 45 minutes. Serve warm with vegetables surrounding the meat.

The Case House Almond Sauce

(yield: ½ gallon; adjust portions by fourths according to amount of chicken being served)
2 cups almond slivers
1 tablespoon butter
6 cups chicken stock
¼ teaspoon white pepper
2 cups cream

Sauté almonds in butter until golden brown. Add chicken stock and pepper and bring to a low simmer. Add cream while whisking the mixture. Allow to simmer for 45 minutes and thicken with a Milders Inn–style roux. Serve as a topping to roasted chicken.

The Case House Brown Gravy

(yield: 4 gallons; an alternative to the Milders Inn Milk Gravy; suggested for use with beef)
4 cups onions, chopped in food processor
4 cups carrots, chopped in food processor
4 cups celery, chopped in food processor
4 teaspoons white pepper
6 bay leaves
1 teaspoon thyme
6 tablespoons Kitchen Bouquet browning sauce
½ cup butter
4 gallons beef stock

Sauté vegetables and seasonings in butter. Add in beef stock and simmer for 45 minutes. Thicken with Milders Inn–style roux after removing bay leaves.

The Case House Giblet Gravy

(yield: 4 gallons; an alternative to the Milders Inn Milk Gravy; suggested for use with poultry)

4 cups onions, chopped in food processor
4 cups carrots, chopped in food processor
4 cups celery, chopped in food processor
4 teaspoons white pepper
6 bay leaves
1 teaspoon thyme
butter
4 gallons turkey stock

Sauté vegetables and seasonings in butter. Add turkey stock and simmer for 45 minutes. Thicken with Milders Inn–style roux after removing bay leaves.

The Case House Honey Glaze

(yield: ¾ gallon; suggested for use with ham)

½ gallon honey
1 teaspoon pumpkin pie spice
¼ teaspoon ground cloves
4 cups corn syrup
2 cups brown sugar

Simmer all ingredients on very low heat until sugar dissolves.

The Case House Mushroom Whiskey Sauce

(yield: 2 gallons)

6 cups fresh mushrooms, quartered
2 large onions, julienned
2 tablespoons garlic, minced
1½ teaspoons black pepper
2 tablespoons fresh thyme, minced
½ cup butter
2 cups whiskey
6 quarts pork stock

Sauté mushrooms, onions, garlic, pepper and thyme in butter. Add whiskey and stir well. Add stock and simmer for 45 minutes. Thicken with Milders Inn–style roux.

The Case House Roasted Reds Butter

(yield: 3 pounds)

3 pounds butter
½ cup garlic
1½ teaspoons basil
1½ teaspoons oregano
2 tablespoons thyme
2 teaspoons rosemary
1 tablespoon salt
2 tablespoons black pepper
3 tablespoons paprika

Add all ingredients to a stock pot and cook thoroughly until garlic is tender.

Breading, Seasonings, Marinades and Batters

The Case House Trout Breading

(could also be used on other types of fish)

1 tablespoon sage
3 pounds Japanese bread crumbs
1 cup dried parsley
2 tablespoons black pepper
3 tablespoons dry thyme
3 tablespoons dry oregano
3 tablespoons dry basil
2 teaspoons rosemary
3 tablespoons onion powder
2 tablespoons garlic powder
3 tablespoons dill weed
2 tablespoons salt

Mix all ingredients together and dredge fresh trout through the mix before baking or deep frying.

The Case House Fritters

4 cups yellow cornmeal
4 cups pancake batter
2 cups water
2 cups creamed corn

Mix all ingredients together and preheat oil in a deep fryer to 325 degrees. Drop the batter by the spoonful into the fryer, cooking for 2 to 4 minutes until golden. Turn the fritters once during the frying process. Drain the grease on paper towels before serving.

The Case House Seasoned Flour and Fried Frog Legs

Egg Wash:
2 eggs
2 tablespoons mayonnaise
1 tablespoon cornstarch
1 tablespoon lemon juice

Flour:
4 cups flour
3 tablespoons salt
1 tablespoon black pepper
1 teaspoon white pepper
1 teaspoon onion powder

Take 2 pounds of frog legs and, after cleaning, place in a shallow, oblong dish. Whisk together the egg wash ingredients and pour over the frog legs. Chill in refrigerator for 30 minutes. Heat fryer oil to 365 degrees and dredge the frog legs through the seasoned flour mixture. Fry for 7 to 8 minutes until the frog legs are golden brown.

The Case House Half Chicken Marinade

(yield: 2 gallons)

2 cups white vinegar
3 cans Wiedemann's beer (or favorite beer if Wiedemann's isn't available)
1½ gallons water
2 lemons, squeezed
2 onions, sliced

Mix all ingredients in a clean five-gallon bucket and then place chicken in the bucket to marinate before cooking.

The Case House General Breading Mix

(adjusted for family use)

10 cups flour
3 tablespoons salt
5 teaspoons white pepper
5 tablespoons black pepper
5 teaspoons onion powder
5 cups cornmeal

Mix together in large silver bowl and store in a white square bucket for future use on various meats.

The Case House Wedge Salt

3 ounces salt
2 tablespoons white pepper
2 tablespoons garlic powder
4 tablespoons onion powder

Mix all ingredients and serve as an alternative to regular salt.

MISCELLANEOUS VEGETABLE RECIPES AND DRESSINGS

The Case House Stewed Tomatoes

(yield: 1 gallon; adjusted for family use)

1 large onion, diced
½ cup butter
1 10-pound can tomatoes
1 teaspoon basil
¼ cup sugar
1 teaspoon black pepper

Sauté onions in butter until tender. Place rest of ingredients in a saucepan, simmering the tomatoes for 30 minutes.

The Case House Whipped Potatoes

(yield: ½ gallon; recipe adjusted for family use; can be served as an alternative to Mom Milders's potatoes and milk gravy)

4 pounds potatoes
½ cup melted butter
2 cups warm whole milk
¼ cup sour cream
½ tablespoon salt
¼ tablespoon white pepper

Steam potatoes for 45 minutes and then put in a mixer with paddle and beat on speed three until potatoes are fluffy. Add in the liquids and season.

The Case House Stewed Apples

(yield: 1 gallon; adjusted for family use)

5 pounds apples, peeled and sliced
¾ cup sugar
1 cup brown sugar
⅛ cup butter
½ tablespoon cinnamon
½ tablespoon nutmeg

Mix all ingredients together in a large bowl. Place in a glass baking dish and bake in oven at 350 degrees for 30 minutes.

The Case House Green Beans

(yield: ½ gallon; adjusted for family use and prepared fresh from the garden just as they were at the Milders Inn)

¼ cup onion
3 slices bacon
¼ cup bacon fat
¼ cup butter
5 pounds freezer beans (see freezer recipe from Mom Milders's tips in Chapter 8)
¼ tablespoon salt
½ teaspoon black pepper

Sauté onions and bacon in butter until tender. Cook beans until tender and strain juice and seasonings in a stock pot and bring to a boil. Add the cooked, strained beans into the stockpot mixture and cook for 30 minutes.

The Case House Sage Dressing

(yield: ¾ gallon; adjusted for family size portions)

3 pounds bread, cubed
½ gallon chicken stock
4 eggs, beaten
1½ tablespoons sage
¾ teaspoon poultry seasoning
1 tablespoon salt
½ tablespoon black pepper
1½ tablespoons parsley, chopped
3 cups celery, chopped
3 cups onion, diced
¾ cup butter, melted

Place bread cubes in a bowl. Mix all remaining ingredients and then pour over the bread. Mix thoroughly by hand and place in a well-sprayed pan.

Cover with foil and bake for 1 hour at 350 degrees. Take foil off and bake an additional 15 minutes. Serve when internal temperature of dressing has reached 160 degrees.

BREADS AND MUFFINS

The Case House Sugar Top Muffins

(Yield: 18 muffins)

2 cups flour
2 cups quick-cooking oats
1½ cups brown sugar
1½ teaspoons baking powder
1½ teaspoons baking soda
2 eggs, beaten
1½ cups milk
⅔ cup oil
1 cup chopped walnuts

Topping:
6 teaspoons sugar
6 teaspoons cinnamon

Combine flour, oats, sugar, powder and soda and set aside. Combine eggs, milk and oil; add to dry ingredients and stir until moistened. Fold in nuts. Using black-handled ice cream scoop, fill well-greased muffin cups with one level scoop of batter. Sprinkle tops with sugar and cinnamon. Bake at 325 degrees for 25 minutes or until toothpick comes out clean.

The Case House Raspberry Muffins

(yield: 15 muffins; cut ingredients in fourths for family use)

¾ cup flour
¾ teaspoon baking powder
½ teaspoon baking soda
¼ teaspoon salt

½ cup butter, softened
1 cup sugar
2 eggs
¾ cup sour cream
¾ teaspoon vanilla
¾ cup raspberries (can use frozen if fresh not available, but drain juice if doing so)

Topping:
¼ teaspoon cinnamon
¼ teaspoon nutmeg
1½ tablespoons sugar

Sift flour, powder, soda and salt together and set aside. In a large bowl, beat butter for 30 seconds, then add sugar and beat until fluffy. Beat in eggs, sour cream and vanilla and stir in dry ingredients until just moistened. Fold in berries. Using black-handled ice cream scoop, fill muffin cups. Mix cinnamon, nutmeg and sugar and sprinkle on top of muffin batter. Bake at 350 degrees for 20 minutes.

The Case House Zucchini Bread

(yield: 2 loaves; cut ingredients in fourths for family use)

2 cups zucchini, cubed and unpeeled
1 cup oil
4 eggs
2 tablespoons vanilla
3 cups flour
2 cups sugar
1 teaspoon baking soda
1 tablespoon cinnamon
1 teaspoon salt
1 cup walnuts, chopped

Combine ½ cup of zucchini, ¼ cup oil, 1 egg and ½ tablespoon of vanilla. Mix in blender and then repeat the process three more times (for a total of four) until above quantities are mixed. In a separate large bowl, combine all dry ingredients and add nuts. Pour equally into 2 greased, floured and lined loaf pans. Bake at 325 degrees for 1 hour or until baked through. Remove from pan and cool before serving.

The Case House Lemon Poppy Seed Bread

(yield: 2 loaves; cut ingredients in fourths for family use)

2 cups sugar
1 cup butter, softened
4 eggs
zest of two lemons
3 cups flour
2 teaspoons baking powder
1 teaspoon salt
4 tablespoons poppy seeds
1 cup milk

Mix ingredients in the order given. Pour into greased and floured loaf pans. Bake at 325 degrees for 45 minutes and test with toothpick for doneness. Bread is done when toothpick comes out clean. Cool before serving.

The Case House Cranberry Orange Nut Bread

(yield: 2 loaves; cut ingredients in fourths for family use)

4½ cups flour
1⅛ cups sugar
1½ tablespoons baking powder
1½ teaspoons salt
¾ teaspoon baking soda
1½ cups orange juice
¾ cup butter, melted
3 eggs, beaten
2 cups cranberry relish
1 orange for zest
¾ cup nuts, chopped

Mix dry ingredients and combine orange juice, butter, eggs, relish and zest. Stir into dry ingredients just until moistened. Add nuts. Pour into greased, lined and floured loaf pans. Bake at 325 degrees for 1 hour. Test for doneness. When toothpick comes out clean, bread is done. Cool before serving.

The Case House Buttermilk Biscuits

(yield: 30 large biscuits; cut recipe in fourths for smaller batch)

10 cups flour
3¾ teaspoons salt
3½ teaspoons baking soda
10 teaspoons baking powder
1¼ cups butter
3¾ cups buttermilk

Sift all dry ingredients together and then cut butter into half-inch cubes. Using pastry cutter, incorporate butter into dry ingredients until mixture resembles a coarse cornmeal. Add buttermilk and mix just enough to make dough. Don't over mix. Knead fifteen times until dough is soft and elastic but not sticky. Roll into a half-inch sheet and cut biscuits with stock base container. Place on a well-greased baking sheet and brush with melted butter. Bake at 350 degrees for 10 to 12 minutes. Remove from oven and brush with butter again.

The Case House Corn Bread

(yield: 60 muffins; cut ingredients in fourths for smaller batch)

6 cups flour
4 teaspoons baking soda
5 tablespoons and 1 teaspoon baking powder
1½ cups sugar
2 tablespoons salt
6 cups cornmeal
½ teaspoon nutmeg
12 eggs, beaten
6 cups buttermilk
1 cup butter, melted
¼ cup bacon fat

Sift flour, soda, powder, sugar and salt. Add cornmeal and nutmeg. Stir eggs, buttermilk, butter and fat. Fill five muffin pans using black-handled ice cream scoop, or fill one large baking sheet and grease both with vegetable spray. Bake at 375 degrees for 10 to 12 minutes.

The Case House Pumpkin Nut Muffins/Bread

(yield: 4 dozen muffins/8 loaves; cut ingredients in fourths for smaller batch)

13 cups flour
8 teaspoons baking soda
6 teaspoons salt
6 teaspoons cinnamon
4 teaspoons nutmeg
12 cups sugar
8 cups pumpkin
16 eggs
4 cups vegetable oil
18 ounces walnuts, chopped

For bread: Mix all ingredients as listed for full batch of batter. Combine dry ingredients (except sugar) and set aside. Mix sugar, pumpkin, eggs and oil in a bowl. Fold in dry ingredients until blended and fold in nuts gently. Pour into greased and floured bread pans. Bake at 325 degrees for 1 hour and 20 minutes. Test with toothpick until it comes out clean to ensure that the bread is done.

For muffins: Mix half of bread ingredients to yield a half batch of batter. Prepare as listed above. Using black-handled ice cream scoop, fill muffin cups with one scoop of batter. Bake at 325 degrees for 25 minutes; use toothpick to make sure muffins are done.

The Case House Strawberry and Cream Bread

(yield: 8 loaves; cut ingredients in fourths for smaller batch)

4 cups butter, softened
6 cups sugar
16 eggs
4 cups sour cream
8 teaspoons vanilla
14 cups flour
4 teaspoons baking powder
4 teaspoons baking soda
4 teaspoons salt
2 teaspoons cinnamon

6 cups fresh strawberries, chopped
6 cups walnuts, toasted

Cream butter and sugar until fluffy. Beat in eggs one at a time. Add sour cream and vanilla and mix well. Combine dry ingredients and then stir into creamed mixture until just moistened. Fold in berries and 4 cups nuts. Pour into greased and floured loaf pans and sprinkle with 2 cups remaining nuts. Bake at 325 degrees for 1 hour or until inserted toothpick comes out clean. Cool 10 minutes in pan and transfer to rack to completely cool before serving.

Desserts

The fruits used to make the following desserts were either grown by Tully Milders in the Case House garden or were purchased from local farmers. This practice of using only farm-fresh ingredients for cakes and pies was handed down to Tully through his family, originally coming from Mom Milders.

The Case House Whipped Cream

(yield: 1 quart)

½ quart heavy cream
1 cup powdered sugar
½ teaspoon vanilla

Place all ingredients in a small bowl and use a hand mixer to whip until stiff peaks form. For a variation, use 1 cup of brown sugar in place of the powdered sugar and add a pinch of cinnamon. Use for topping on the Case House desserts.

The Case House Apple Pie

(yield: 5 pies; adjust ingredients in fourths for fewer pies)

5 pre-purchased, frozen pie shells, thawed
9 pounds apples, peeled and sliced
2 pounds sugar
6 tablespoons cornstarch

½ tablespoon salt
½ tablespoon cinnamon
1 tablespoon nutmeg
egg whites for brushing crust

Topping:
2 cups brown sugar
1⅓ cups flour
1⅓ cups softened butter
For topping: Crumble together all ingredients using a pastry blender.

For pie, combine all ingredients, crimp edges of crust and brush with egg whites. Fill the five shells and cover with the topping. Bake at 350 degrees for 30 minutes, leaving pies uncovered. Remove pies from oven, place the pies on a baking sheet and cover all the pies with foil. Bake another 30 minutes until golden brown.

The Case House Fruit Cobbler

(adjusted for family use)

1 cup sugar
½ cup corn syrup
¼ teaspoon cinnamon
⅛ teaspoon nutmeg
¼ pound butter
1 cup juice from fruit (if using fresh fruit, add water instead)
¼ teaspoon lemon juice
1 teaspoon cornstarch
¼ cup water
*2½ pounds fresh fruit (**note can use frozen fruit cocktail if fresh fruit isn't available; if frozen fruit is used, save the juice in separate bowl)*
¼ of a batch of biscuit dough

Combine sugar, corn syrup, cinnamon, nutmeg, butter, juice/water and lemon juice in saucepan. Bring to a boil. If using peaches, do not add to the mixture until the butter has melted. Add cornstarch thickening (water and starch blend until as thick as a heavy gravy). If using berries, add them in after the mixture has thickened. Return fruits to a boil, but do not let them stick or burn. Roll half of biscuit dough to cover bottom and halfway up the side of a baking pan. Bake at 350 degrees for 5 minutes. Roll other half of dough to cover top using a rolling pin. Pour hot fruit over baked biscuit bottom crust in pan. Cover with top crust, make slits, brush with melted butter and then sprinkle with sugar. Bake at 325 degrees for 20 minutes.

The Case House Bread Pudding

(adjusted for family use)

½ cup butter, melted
½ pound bread, torn into loose pieces
4 eggs
¼ pound sugar
¼ teaspoon salt
¼ teaspoon vanilla
1 teaspoon cinnamon
1 teaspoon nutmeg
½ cup red raisins
½ cup golden raisins
2½ cups milk, scalded

Pour melted butter over torn bread. Mix eggs, sugar, salt, vanilla, spices and raisins. Add milk and pour over bread. Preheat a water pan to 350 degrees. Place bread mixture in a four-inch hotel pan, cover with foil, set cooking pan in water and bake for 1 hour. Turn heat down to 300 degrees and bake for 15 minutes longer. Uncover and bake another 15 minutes until the bread pudding has an internal temperature of 160 degrees.

The Case House Carrot Cake

(yield: 1 nine-inch cake)

2 cups flour
2 teaspoons cinnamon
1 teaspoon baking powder
¼ teaspoon salt
⅔ cup butter softened
1 cup sugar

3 eggs
⅔ cup milk
3 medium carrots, grated
½ cup walnuts, coarsely chopped

Frosting:
½ cup butter, softened
4 ounces cream cheese, softened
1 teaspoon vanilla
2½ cups confectioners' sugar

Topping:
¼ cup walnuts, finely chopped
2 tablespoons brown sugar

Grease, line and dust a nine-inch cake pan. Mix dry ingredients and beat together butter and sugar until fluffy. Add eggs one at a time, beating well. At low speed, alternate dry ingredients and milk into butter mixture. Stir in carrots and nuts. Pour into prepared cake pan and bake at 325 degrees for 40 minutes. Cool cake in pan for 10 minutes and remove to rack to cool completely. For frosting, beat butter and cream cheese at medium speed until smooth and then beat in vanilla. Beat in sugar until well blended. Mix nuts and brown sugar together for topping. Spread icing over top and sides of cake and sprinkle top with nut topping mixture.

The Case House Raspberry Jam Bars

4 cups flour
4 teaspoons baking powder
2 cups butter, softened
8 eggs
4 teaspoons milk
4 cups raspberry jam
4 cups sugar
4 teaspoons vanilla
1 cup butter, melted
2 pounds chopped nuts

Pastry blend flour, powder and 2 cups butter. Stir in 4 eggs and milk. Roll dough evenly onto full greased baking sheet and spread jam over dough. Mix sugar, remaining 4 eggs and vanilla and slowly add warm melted butter and then the nuts. Spread mixture over jam that has been placed in a baking pan and bake at 350 degrees for 20 minutes. Allow to cool, then cut into 60 6x10 bars.

The Case House Apple Dapple Cake

(yield: 1 fluted cake)

3 eggs, well beaten
1½ cups oil
2 teaspoons vanilla
2 cups sugar
2¾ cups flour
1 teaspoon baking soda
1 teaspoon salt
½ teaspoon nutmeg
1 teaspoon cinnamon
¼ cup flour
3 cups apples, chopped
1 cup nuts, chopped
1 cup coconut

Topping:
⅓ cup butter
1 cup brown sugar
¼ cup milk
1 teaspoon vanilla

Beat eggs well and add oil, vanilla and sugar. Sift 2¾ cups of flour, baking soda, salt, nutmeg and cinnamon together. Add to egg mixture. Mix additional ¼ cup flour, apples, nuts and coconut and fold into cake batter. Pour into fluted tube pan and bake at 350 degrees for 1 hour until tester comes out clean. Mix topping ingredients in small saucepan and boil for 2 to 3 minutes. Pour hot topping over cake about 5 minutes after removing cake from oven.

The Case House Derby Pie

(yield: 3 pies; cut in thirds for one pie)

3 pie shells, thawed
6 eggs
3 cups sugar
½ cup flour
1½ cups butter, melted (do not use margarine)
3 cups chocolate chips
3 cups chopped pecans
5 tablespoons Kentucky bourbon
2 teaspoons vanilla

Crimp edges of pie shells, poke holes in bottom of shell with pastry bag tip and brush with egg whites. Beat eggs, sugar, flour and butter in mixer with paddle. Add chips, pecans, bourbon and vanilla and fold with spatula. Pour into shells and bake at 325 degrees for 40 minutes.

The Case House Buttercream Frosting

(for use on favorite cakes or breads)

1 pound butter, softened
½ teaspoon salt
2 teaspoons vanilla
16 cups confectioners' sugar
3 cups heavy cream

Blend butter, salt and vanilla in a large mixer bowl. Slowly add sugar, then add cream. Beat for 5 minutes. Can be stored in refrigerator for up to seven days.

EPILOGUE

In 2005, four historical markers were placed around the city of Fairfield, Ohio, so citizens could remember those buildings that were significant to their history. Fairfield councilman Howard Dirksen told the *Fairfield Echo* that the markers were installed in honor of the city's fiftieth anniversary. He said that history is as important to Fairfield as the present, bringing perspective and educating citizens about their past. One of the markers was installed at 590 Nilles Road, now the site of a CVS pharmacy and the former site of the Milders Inn. The marker, along with those representing the former Symmes Tavern, the former McCormick Farm and the former City Administration Building, remain in place today, highlighting the Symmes Corner neighborhood where the Milders family made their living and that still defines the city's downtown. For the remaining members of the Milders family, the placement of the marker is the source of much family pride, as it not only offers an important look back at their own family tree but also reminds each of them of the integral role that Jake, Mom, Ray and the historic Milders Inn played in Fairfield, as well as in the entire Butler County community.

Likewise, one of a series of murals painted by nationally known artist Eric Henn is located on the outside of the Fairfield post office, paying tribute to the Milders Inn by highlighting a waving Jake Milders standing outside his famous restaurant. The mural reminds everyone who passes by that the Milders family has made a major impact on Fairfield's and the regional culture—a legacy that continues and will remain in place for many years to come.

The site of the Milders Inn today with the historical marker placed in 2005 as part of Fairfield, Ohio's fiftieth anniversary celebration. *Captured Beauty Photography.*

Today, as the city celebrates its sixtieth anniversary, the Milderses and their story continue to highlight a significant part of Fairfield's history. A 2015 historical exhibit at Fairfield's Community Arts Center features hundreds of memories, especially those from the late 1930s and early 1940s, when the Reds frequented the inn and the Milderses' home nearby. Bob Pendergrass designed the exhibit and is the previous owner of Ray Milders's former home, having just sold it in the summer of 2015. Pendergrass said that owning that property on what is now called Shady Lane was an important part of his own history:

> *We bought the house in 1972, and though I have made many improvements, including the addition of a garage and family room, I am constantly told about the stories of the 1940 Reds players who used to sleep in my backyard. Even my doctor told me that his father-in-law remembered the players coming to my house, and just owning this piece of history is fantastic and a source of great pride for me.*

The new owners of the Ray Milders home are just as excited about the history of their property and have left much of the patio in its original form. Surprisingly, the area is much smaller than the stories suggest and at most,

Bob Pendergrass, the archivist for the Fairfield Ohio Historical Society, with his 2015 Milders Inn exhibit at the Fairfield Community Arts Center. The exhibit is part of the sixtieth-anniversary celebration of the city. *Captured Beauty Photography.*

could support three to four adult men. It appears that the Reds players who chose to sleep outside in the cool night air likely slept on the grass instead of the brick. Likewise, one can almost hear the ghostly laughter of the former Reds players who stayed there and the giggles of a young "Petie" Milders as she served in the wedding parties of Harry Craft and Frank McCormick. Though the young children who now play at the home have no idea about the history of their backyard, for those who have been around long enough to know the story of the Milders Inn, the former Fairfield home of Ray Milders serves as a shrine to the memories of the city's most famous family.

NOTE FROM THE AUTHOR

The anecdotes in this book are compiled from Milders family oral histories, newspaper accounts and various other sources that reported actual historical events. While a single story may have multiple interpretations, the inclusion of each demonstrates its importance to the Milders Inn and to the overall family story. Though the history of the Milders family and their inn is broader than most, covering 165 years between 1850 and 2015, it is important to travel the many side roads where the story leads. One cannot gain a full appreciation of the importance of the inn and its relationship to the local culture without doing so. With a connection to sports, music, business development, the 1913 flood and even great food, it is my hope that readers will gain a deeper understanding of how one restaurant can truly define a generation. In addition, all cooking tips, recipes and preferred cookware recommendations come from the experience of the Milders family and have not been tested by the author. As such, readers are advised to utilize any culinary recommendations at their own discretion.

BIBLIOGRAPHY

Alexander, Scott. "Hitches Happy Harmonists." The Red Hot Jazz Archive. www.redhotjazz.com.

AME History. "World War II Rationing on the U.S. Homefront." www.amehistory.org/exhibits/events/rationing.htm.

Ancestry.com. "Frank J. Doellman." www.ancestry.com/cgi-bin/sse.dll?db=1900USFedCen&indiv=try&h=38932105.

———. "Margaret Lail Milders." www.ancestry.com/cgi-bin/sse.dll?db1930USFedCen&indiv=try&h=38932105.

———. "Ray Milders." www.ancestry.com/cgi-bin/sse.dll?db1930USFedCen&Indiv=try&h=38932105.

———. "Ray Milders." www.ancestry.com/cgi-bin/sse.dll?db1940USFedCen&Indiv=try&h=38932105.

Arnold, Horace. "Modern Machine—Shop Economics, Part II." *Engineering Magazine*, 1896, 11.

Axelrod, Alan. *International Encyclopedia of Secret Societies and Fraternal Orders.* New York: Facts on File Inc., 1997.

Baseball Almanac. "Billy Myers Stats." www.baseball-almanac.com/players/player.php?p=myersbi01.

———. "Oldest Living Baseball Players." www.baseball-almanac.com/players/Oldest_Living_Baseball_Players.php.

Baseball Hall of Fame. "Ernie Lombardi." www.baseballhall.org/hof/lombardi-ernie.

———. "Waite Hoyt." www.baseballhall.org/hof/hoyt-waite.

Baseball Reference. "Ernie Lombardi." www.baseball-reference.com/players/l/lombaer01.shtml.

———. "Frank McCormick." www.baseball-reference.com/players/m/mccorfr01.shtml.

———. "Harry Craft." www.baseball-reference.com/players/c/craftha01.shtml.

———. "Herm Winningham." www.baseball-reference.com/players/w/winnihe01.shtml.

———. "Lew Riggs." www.baseball-reference.com/players/r/riggsle01.shtml.

———. "Willard Hershberger." www.baseball-reference.com/players/h/hershwi01.shtml.

Beeler, Louise. "This and That, About Hamilton, Yesterday and Today." *Hamilton Journal and Daily News*, December 1, 1962.

Bennigan's. "The Menu." www.bennigans.com/bennigans-menu.

Benzing, Esther. *Fairfield, Ohio*. Mt. Healthy, OH: Porter Printing Inc., May 1978.

Biography. "Dick Powell Biography." www.biography.com/people/dick-powell-9542102.

Blount, Jim. "Butler County Place Names, 'Milders Inn.'" Jim Blount Resources. www.lanepl.org/research/local-history/genealogy-jim-blount-resources.

———. *Butler County's Greatest Weather Disaster—March 1913*. Hamilton, OH: Past/Present/Press, 2002.

———. "Coliseum Home for Sports and Entertainment." *Hamilton Journal News*, December 16, 1991.

———. *A History of the Prohibition Era in Hamilton and Butler County, Ohio, Little Chicago*. Vol. 1: *The Early Years, 1919–1927*. Hamilton, OH: Past/Present/Press, 1997.

———. *A History of the Prohibition Era in Hamilton and Butler County, Ohio, Little Chicago*. Vol. 2: *The Deadly Years, 1928–1942*. Hamilton, OH: Past/Present/Press, 1997.

Bogan, Dallas. *Warren County, Ohio and Beyond*. N.p.: Heritage Press, 1979.

Butler County Ohio. "Property Search." www.propertysearch.butlercountyohio.org/butler/search/commonsearch.aspx?mode.

Campbell, Polly. "The Case House, Dining Review." *Cincinnati Enquirer*, April 18, 1997.

CareerPlanning.com. "Average Salary of an American Boilermaker in 2015." www.careerplanning.com.

Carmichael, Hoagy. *Sometimes I Wonder*. New York: Farrar, Straus, and Giroux, 1965.

Cincinnati Enquirer. "Jacob Milders Obituary." January 6, 1934.

Cincinnati Reds Hall of Fame & Museum. "The First Big Red Machine, the 1940 Cincinnati Reds." www.cincinnati.reds.mlb.com/cin/hof/about/index.jsp?loc=1940reds.

City of Fairfield, Ohio. "History of Fairfield." www.fairfield-city.org/live/history.cfm.

Cummins, George. Cummins Room Holdings, Cummins Photo Collection, Lane Public Library, Hamilton, Ohio. www.lanepl.org/research/local-history/genealogy-cummins-room-holdings.

Dine.com. "Attractions Restaurant & Pub." www.dine.com/restaurants/Attractions-Restaurant-Pub-Oxford-Ohio-48070.html.

Eaton, Ercel. "Missives Bring Bits of Past into Focus." *Hamilton Journal News*, November 9, 1997.

———. "Petie Murphy Won't Forget Reds' 1940 Pennant Winners." *Hamilton Journal News*, August 29, 1995.

———. "Return to Yesteryear." *Hamilton Journal News*, August 11, 2002.

Ebay.com. "Red River Cattle Co. Red River Saloon Menu, Hamilton, Ohio 1980's6PoundSteak."www.ebay.com/itm/141772711408?mwBanner=1.

Epodunk.com. "Profile for Somerville, Ohio." www.epodunk.com/cgi-bin/geninfo.php?loclndex=274912.

Fairfield, Ohio. "Post Office Murals." www.fairfield-city.org/arts/postoffice.cfm.

FCC Digplanet. "WCKY." www.digplanet.com/wiki/WCKY_(AM).

The Federal Bureau of Investigation. "Famous Cases and Criminals—John Dillinger." www.fbi.gov/about-us/history/famous-cases/john-dillinger.

Find a Grave. "Anna Heet Doellman." www.findagrave.com/cgi-bin/fg.cgi?page=gsr&gsfn=Doellman&gsfn=Anna&gs.

———. "Frank Doellman." www.findagrave.com/cgi-bin/fg.cgi?page=gsr&gsfn=Frank&gsmn=J&Gsln-do.

——— "Jacob Milders." www.findagrave.com/cgi-bin/fg.cgi?page=gsr&gsfn=jacob&gsmn=&gsln=mil.

———. "Mary A. Milders." www.findagrave.com/cgi-bin/fg.cgi?page=gsr&gsfn=marya&gsmn=&gsln=mil.

FirstWorldWard.com. "Women and World War I—Women in the Workforce: Temporary Men." www.firstworldwar.com/features/womenww1_four.htm.

Franklin, Benjamin. *The Political Thought of Benjamin Franklin*. Edited by Ralph Ketchum. Indianapolis, IN: Hackett Publishing, 2003.

Hamilton Journal News. "Jacob Milders, Prominent Citizen, Is Called." Obituary, January 6, 1934.

Hoel, Nellie. "Withrow Family History." Family stories passed down to Teri Horsley, 1980–2015.

Holbrock, Mable. "Milders Inn Popular Place in 1920's." *Fairfield Sun*, October 7, 1981.

———. "Milders Inn Was a First Class Restaurant." *Fairfield Sun*, April 11, 1979.
———. "Milders Inn Was Frequented by Reds' Stars." *Fairfield Sun*, February 1980.
———. "Milders' Was Famous for Chicken and Steak." *Fairfield Sun*, April 18, 1979.
———. "Milders' Was Frequented by Reds' Stars." *Fairfield Sun*, April 25, 1979.
Horstman, Barry. "Powell Crosley Jr.: Innovator, Sportsman Dreamed Big." *Cincinnati Post*, April 8, 1999.
Hover, John, Joseph Barnes, Walter Jones, Charlotte Conover, Willard Wright and Clayton Leiter. "Memoirs of the Miami Valley." www.rootsweb.ancestry.com/ohbutler/001/49.html.
IMDB. "Ashton Kutcher." www.imdb.com/name/nm0005110/?ref_=nv_sr_1.
———. "Courtney Love." www.imdb.com/name/nm0001482/?ref_=nv_sr_1.
———. "Garret Dillahunt." www.imdb.com/name/nm0226813/?ref_=nv_sr_1.
———. "James Franco." www.imdb.com/name/nm0290556/?ref_=fn_al_nm_1.
———. "Josh Hutcherson." www.imdb.com/name/nm1242688/?ref_=nv_sr_1.
———. "Zoe Levin." www.imdb.com/name/nm4534201/?ref_=nv_sr_1.
Immigration to the United States. "Dutch Immigrants." www.immigrationtounitedstates.org.
Jones, Mike. "Local Memories of Hoagy Carmichael." *Hamilton Journal News*, December 31, 1981.
Jones, Richard. "Famous Hamilton Fried Chicken Rooted in History." *Hamilton Journal News*, July 21, 2013.
Kieswetter, Sue. "1913 Flood, Milders Inn Are Focus of Fairfield's Sunbonnet Days." July 25, 2014. www.local.cincinnati.com/share/story/216613.
Kinder, Jill, Dave Crouch, Jeff Kursman and Dena Morsch. *Fairfield, Ohio: From the Pioneers to Our Golden Years, 1955–2005*. Fairfield, OH: City of Fairfield, 2005.
Kursman, Laura. "A Bit of History Repeating." *Cincy Magazine*, October–November 2013. www.cincymagazine.com/Main/Articles/Dining_3910.aspx.
Manuel, Dave. "Inflation Calculator." www.davemanuel.com/inflation-calculator.
McClure, Rusty. *Crosley: Two Brothers and a Business Empire that Transformed the Nation*. Cincinnati, OH: Clerisy Press, 2006.
McDulin, Bill. "Got a Minute?" *Hamilton Journal News*, 1974.
McNutt, Randy. "Hamilton Reviving Little Chicago." *Cincinnati Enquirer*, November 12, 1999.
Media Heritage. "Dick Bray." www.mediaheritage.com/dick-bray.

Milders, Mary. Various recipes. Milders Family Archives.
Milders, Ray. Personal letter to historian Esther Benzing, 1978.
Milders, Tully. Oral history interview with Teri Horsley. June 30, 2015; July 6, 2015; August 10, 2015; August 24, 2015; October 14, 2015.
Miller Center. "American President, Zachary Taylor." University of Virginia. www.millercenter.org/president/taylor.
Nack, William. "The Razor's Edge." *Sports Illustrated*, May 6, 1991.
Newspaper.com. "The Journal News." *Hamilton Daily News*, account of Turkey Joe Jacobs's murder, May 28, 1929. www.newspaper.com/image/36128736.
———. "The Journal News." *Hamilton Evening Journal*, account of Turkey Joe Jacobs's murder, May 28, 1929. www.newspaper.com/image/23124320.
Newton, Jim. "Angry Words Written 40 Years Ago by Hamilton Man; Career Is Linked with Big Names in Famed Music Era." *Hamilton Journal News*, October 1965.
Nowlin, Bill. *Spahn, Sain, and Teddy Ballgame: Boston's (Almost) Perfect Baseball Summer of 1948*. Boston: Rounder Books, 2008.
Ohio History Central. "German Ohioans." www.ohiohistorycentral.org/w/German_Ohioans?rec+592.
PartSelect.com. "The Rise of the Electric Home Appliance." www.partselect.com/JustForFun/Rise-Of-The-Electric-Home-Appliance.aspx.
Pendergrass, Bob. Oral history interview with Teri Horsley, October 16, 2015.
Pitman, Michael. "Markers Tell Fairfield's Downtown History." *Fairfield Echo*, October 6, 2005.
———. "Noting the Past to Help Build a Better Future." *Hamilton Journal News*, October 11, 2005.
Rentschler, Bill. Personal letter to Petie Milders Murphy, August 21, 2002.
RetroCincinnati.com. "Powell Crosley." www.retrocincinnati.com/Topics/Powell-Crosley-Jr.
Richard's Pizza. "Richard's Pizza History Timeline." www.richardspizza.com.
Ruhl, Valentine. "My Life of Valentine Ruhl." Diary of the author, July 4, 1862.
Ryan, Don. Oral history interview with Teri Horsley, October 14, 2015.
Safeandvault.com. "Mosler Safe Company." www.safeandvault.com/faq/115-gsa-containers/705-mosler-safe-company.
Schaff, Phillip. "Protestantism." New Schaff–Herzog Encyclopedia of Religious Knowledge IX, 1914.
Sloneker, Marlene. Oral history interview with Teri Horsley, July 6, 2015.
SouthernFriedChickenRecipe.com. "History of Fried Chicken through the Ages." www.southernfriedchickenrecipe.com/articles/history-of-fried-chicken-through-the-ages.

Sudhalter, Richard. *Bix: Man and Legend.* New York: Arlington House, 1974.

Swope, Tom. "Hershberger Suicide, No Unpremeditated Act." *Sporting News*, August 8, 1940.

USeconomy.com. "The Value of a Dollar in 1920." www.useconomy.com/inflation.

U.S. Embassy. "Average U.S. Salary in 1900." www.usembassy.com/deletexts/his/e-prices/.htm.

Wigley, Brian. *Willard Hershberger and the Legacy of Suicide.* N.p.: National Pastime (Society for American Baseball Research), 2000.

Williams, Geoff. *Washed Away: How the Great Flood of 1913, America's Most Widespread Natural Disaster, Terrorized a Nation and Changed It Forever.* New York: Pegasus Books, 2013.

Wilson, Tracey. "The History of Fast Food." www.science.howstuffworks.com/innovation/edible-innovations/fast-food3.htm.

World History Project. "What Happened in 1850." www.worldhistoryproject.org/1850.

INDEX

M

N

O

P

Q

R

S

T

U

V

W

X

Z

ABOUT THE AUTHOR

After ending her career as a radio news reporter and talk show host, Teri Horsley decided to combine her love of writing, history and food to become a freelance food writer and restaurant critic for the Cox Ohio Newspaper Group, as well as for numerous regional magazines. A passion for the "stories behind the food" prompted her to earn her master's degree in public history at Northern Kentucky University in 2015, which ultimately led to her writing this book. Early in her food writing career, Horsley recognized that food and dining make up a huge part of American culture, and she believes the stories like those surrounding the historic Milders Inn often create our desire to connect to our past. Having earned numerous awards and hundreds of publishing credits for her writing and daily talk show, Horsley has also served as a food judge for the Midwest Foodways Alliance state fair project. In addition, her historical writing credits go beyond the world of food, and she was selected by the Kentucky Historical Society to write an educational curriculum explaining the history of slavery in the state. As someone who believes in giving back to her community, Horsley also serves as a planning commissioner in her hometown of Hamilton, Ohio. Her interest in historic preservation and heritage tourism led her to develop and lead a successful Hamilton, Ohio food tour in 2014, and she currently has a National Register nomination pending before the State of Ohio Historic Preservation Commission. In her day job, Horsley serves as a sales representative for Porter Advertising, a locally owned outdoor advertising company. In her spare time, she continues to remain active in the

Cincinnati-area culinary community through her involvement with many special dining and cooking events at the Midwest Culinary Institute, and she remains supportive of her favorite regional restaurants by promoting them through a variety of social media formats. With her love for telling great stories, Horsley is pursuing a second master's degree in film producing from Regent University, with an expected graduation date of 2018. It is her desire to make documentary films about many of the subjects about which she has previously written.